TRUE HISTORY

THE FOUNDERS UNMASKED

BY JENNIFER SABIN

PENGUIN WORKSHOP

PENGUIN WORKSHOP
An imprint of Penguin Random House LLC, New York

First published in the United States of America by Penguin Workshop,
an imprint of Penguin Random House LLC, New York, 2022

CONTENTS

Foreword: A Note from Jennifer Sabin, the Creator of

    True History 4

Introduction: A Note from

    Professor Christopher Sebastian Parker 10

Chapter 1: A Country's Creed 17

Chapter 2: A Complicated Legacy:

    Thomas Jefferson 38

Chapter 3: An American Life: Sally Hemings 57

Chapter 4: Abolitionist or Slaveholder?:

    Alexander Hamilton 73

Chapter 5: "What to the Slave Is the Fourth of July?":

    Frederick Douglass 90

Chapter 6: Flawed Hero: George Washington 104

Chapter 7: Hard History: James Madison and the

    Constitution 123

Further Readings 143

FOREWORD
A NOTE FROM JENNIFER SABIN, THE CREATOR OF TRUE HISTORY

As a radio and television news writer and editor for seventeen years, I was used to a certain pace of work. Broadcast newsrooms are like hospitals: The day can hum along quietly, efficiently—until out of nowhere, a bomb goes off, a plane crashes, or a fire wreaks havoc on a community, and suddenly, you're moving at one hundred miles per hour. The difference, of course, is that reporting the news isn't usually a matter of life or death (unless you're reporting from a war zone).

There is an addictive quality to journalism—waiting or searching for the next story; wondering when the adrenaline rush will come, kicking the newsroom into high gear. In broadcasting, those stories can come fast and furiously, and there isn't always an opportunity to delve into a subject. Thirty seconds might be all you have to report on the deadly tornado that ripped through a small town.

Writing about history forces you to move in the other direction, combing through the lives of the newsmakers of the past and the work of the historians who have tried to make sense of it all. It's a slower pace that requires patience. The mountain of material can be daunting—enormous biographies, detailed historical accounts, online essays, and the letters and financial accounts of an important figure. It's another kind of rush: the joy of uncovering some gem that makes the hours of research worth the trouble, connecting the dots in lives lived hundreds of years ago.

This series doesn't pretend to read all that material or tell every story, each biography in full—not even close. I've approached this series as a journalist, in an effort to locate and piece together some of what we miss when we're told the story of the United States of America. My goal is to point out some of the half-truths and lies we are taught as children and to present history through a more critical lens, in the narratives that are often just a footnote to the text or left out entirely, through the voices that aren't always heard when US students open their history books.

Some Americans prefer to leave those stories out of the text for good, believing that they diminish the United States and teach children to hate their country.

On the contrary, Americans can understand difficult truths about their country and still love it dearly. In the words of the great author James Baldwin, "I love America more than any other country in the world, and, exactly for this reason, I insist on the right to criticize her perpetually."

Who does it serve if we are taught myths rather than facts, if we only hear from the perspective of the oppressors and not the oppressed? If we are only told the part of the story that glorifies the nation's founding and deifies the men who led the way?

The story changes and grows, becomes fuller and more nuanced, when different voices participate. It matters who tells the story, when they tell it, and how they choose to present the facts. Textbooks often present a version of history that is sanitized for young audiences, presented to promote patriotism and American exceptionalism: The idea that the United States, as the greatest country on earth, is a force for good in the world with a unique mission to spread freedom and democracy. In that telling, stories that paint the country in a negative light are often struck from the record.

The True History series seeks to help rectify those shortcomings one subject at a time, through interviews and documentation, perspective, and context.

How does the history of Jim Crow in the United States provide context to the Black Lives Matter movement and the systemic racism that still infects our country? Does the story of the United States' first leaders reach different conclusions when women write about the Founders? (Sometimes, yes.) What happens when an Indigenous person looks back to reflect on how the history of his people in the Americas affects Native American life today? And how does the story of immigration in the United States change when we look at it from new perspectives?

With the True History series, we're looking back, but we're also looking inward at the United States' successes and systemic problems and how the past has delivered the country to the present. We're also looking ahead to how we might take the lessons of history and reorient ourselves in the present to find new ways forward.

We have not shied away from complex language, and I have defined words and explained ideas that can be difficult to understand. And when there is subject matter that some readers will find particularly disturbing, I have given you a "just a heads-up."

The Founders Unmasked sets out *not* to rewrite history but to collect some of the existing facts and growing body of evidence that paint a more honest picture than US kids are usually taught about the men we call Founding Fathers. The purpose is not to tell you how to think about these men but to give you information and tools to ask tough questions and come to your own conclusions. I'm not interested in labeling the Founders heroes or villains. I might knock them off their pedestals at times, but I'm not advocating for their statues to be pulled down or their names to be peeled off the facades of public buildings: It's up to individual communities to decide who stays, who goes.

The objective of this book is to accurately describe aspects of the lives they lived in and out of the spotlight and how their professional declarations, core beliefs, and personal decisions were often in conflict with one another. I have included a chapter devoted to a Black woman whose life was under the control of the Founder who enslaved her, and a Black man who led the abolition movement of a future generation. Their stories deserve to be told, not as footnotes to the Founders' stories but in their own right. Their lives are integral and individual parts of the American story that can help us understand issues of race in the United States today.

I hope you find this book illuminating and thought-provoking. And I hope it sparks discussion and debate in your homes and classrooms, the kinds of conversations I always enjoyed in the newsroom.

INTRODUCTION
A NOTE FROM PROFESSOR
CHRISTOPHER SEBASTIAN PARKER

The United States of America has long been touted as "a shining city on a hill," a beacon of hope for the rest of the world to follow as a model of democracy. And many Americans believe deeply in American exceptionalism: the idea that the United States is a unique force for good and plays a positive role on the world stage. But for many, that belief in an unshakable model democracy was upended on January 6, 2021, when a violent mob of people stormed the Capitol building in an attempt to overturn the results of the 2020 presidential election.

Beyond the physical damage done to the building and

the threat to members of Congress and their staffs is the psychological violence visited on communities of color, especially Black people and Jews. Parading the Confederate battle flag through the halls of the seat of American democracy was a jarring sight. The same can be said for the gear worn by some rioters that suggested the Holocaust was a good thing. They were reminders of the country's racist history, and a wakeup call for some Americans that their country is not quite what they thought it was. That its ideals are based on a myth.

To the extent that the founding myth of America as an exemplar of democracy rests on the character of the men who founded the country, *Founders Unmasked* is a much-needed corrective, one that reconciles the myth of American exceptionalism with the reality of American racism. This book refuses to repeat the half-truths told to American schoolkids for generations: that the Founders were great men, absent flaws of any kind. According to the myth, our relative prosperity, freedom, and status as a global power are products of their wisdom and foresight. Instead, *Founders Unmasked* makes it plain for all to see the full range of the Founders' characters. If the Founders' good qualities are responsible for

American "greatness," surely their character flaws have much to do with our failure to attain the "more perfect union" to which the country claims to aspire.

While giving due credit to the Founders, including their heroism and genius, the book reveals a number of their ethical shortcomings. To begin, a majority of those who signed the Declaration of Independence, the document that declared why the colonists wished to break from Great Britain, owned slaves. Of course, the irony is that the document says that "all men are created equal," and have the right to "life, liberty and the pursuit of happiness." The latter are the principal reasons why the colonies sought to break from Great Britain: So long as the country remained attached to King George, these rights would continue to elude them. Evidently, most of the Founders didn't think these rights extended to Black people.

Consider Thomas Jefferson, the nation's third president, and principal architect of the Declaration of Independence. It's well-known that he owned enslaved persons—up to six hundred in his lifetime. Even so, publicly he railed against the evils of slavery in the Declaration of Independence, saying that King George forced it on the colonists, but this wasn't true: King George never did that. Ultimately it didn't matter; the passage was later removed from the document. The fact that Jefferson "opposed" slavery, even as he fathered six children with Sally Hemings, one of his enslaved people, suggests his dishonesty. He even had a chance to completely outlaw slavery as president, but failed to do so. Yes, on his watch, he banned the importation of slaves from Africa, but he didn't outlaw it. Why? Because he benefited from it. George Washington is another founder who "opposed" slavery but had something to gain by permitting it to continue: economic prosperity. Is this any different from the perpetuation of discrimination and institutional racism?

The American Revolution (1775–1783), taking place during the age of revolution (French: 1789–1799; Haitian: 1791–1804), was an attempt to shed the shackles of the British throne. It's typically billed as an effort to construct a nation where citizenship rested on enlightened ideals such as freedom, equality, and tolerance, not ethnic, religious, or class identity, a common practice in Europe. What *Founders Unmasked* introduces, however, is the possibility that the revolution served as a cover for genocide. Removing or killing indigenous people during the course of the Revolution made room for the American nation to come. What's more, fighting both the British *and* Native Americans helped to galvanize the thirteen colonies into a nation, for they had common enemies. Sound familiar? It should: White nationalism requires enemies as a means of ensuring solidarity.

Founders Unmasked does a great service to American history by illustrating the complexity of the Founders. But it also deserves praise for recovering the voices and lives of those who suffered in antebellum America (1815–1861). For instance, the author takes great care to humanize Jefferson's companion, Sally Hemings. The book documents how they met, the phases of their relationship, and how she may have processed the affair, given when it took place: a span of forty years covering the late eighteenth century to the early nineteenth century, until his death. The book also details her background as a multiracial woman, a portrait fleshed out by way of comments from a son she shared with Jefferson. This chapter makes plain a narrative that continues to the present: the subordination of women of color in the United States.

The book also highlights the agency of Frederick Douglass, offering details of his rise from slavery to one of the major abolitionists of his time. Of course, the highlight of the Douglass chapter is the speech he delivered at Corinthian Hall in 1852. The occasion was a celebration of American freedom: the Fourth of July. Douglass begins the speech with the typical polite salutations to the dignitaries in attendance, after which he launches into the guts of his presentation. In sum, he lets his audience know, in no uncertain terms, that the celebration of the colonies' freedom from British rule means *nothing* to the enslaved person. To expect enslaved people to celebrate it, or to do so (celebrate) in their presence, is cruel, even perverted. In light of the continuing presence of white supremacy, and the burden it imposes on communities of color, it hardly makes sense for them to celebrate America's freedom, when they continue to face violence and institutional racism.

In the final analysis, *Founders Unmasked* is an indispensable resource for those who wish to understand the unvarnished version of the Founders and their legacy. Where their heroism and brilliance laid the foundation for America's position as a world power, their flaws allowed racism and sexism to prevail, preventing the formation of the "more perfect union" set forth in the Declaration of Independence.

CHAPTER 1
A COUNTRY'S CREED

When Thomas Jefferson arrived in Philadelphia in 1776 for the most important summer of his life, he wasn't alone. A fourteen-year-old named Robert Hemings traveled with him from Virginia to the city where thirty-three-year-old Jefferson would write, and sign, the Declaration of Independence. Hemings was a body servant, or valet, to the Virginia plantation owner and future third president of the United States. He helped Jefferson dress and shave. He ran small errands for him. He followed him when he rode horseback and likely brought him his meals. He had no choice but to do whatever he was told: Hemings was one of the many Black people Jefferson enslaved. He was also the half brother of his wife.

While Jefferson drafted one of the most famous documents in US history, Hemings waited on him hand and foot. Maybe it was Hemings who refilled Jefferson's inkwell as he wrote the lofty words of that great document, which declared Americans free from British rule and free to pursue their dreams: "All men are created equal."

Robert Hemings, however, wasn't free to pursue his dreams. Neither were hundreds of thousands of enslaved Africans living in the colonies at the time. As the Patriots fought and died for their freedom from Great Britain and the rule of King George III, they continued to deny freedom to enslaved Africans.

HISTORY RECAP

Colonists were the settlers in British America. *Patriots* were the colonists who fought the British for their freedom. *Loyalists* supported the British cause and did not want to break from Great Britain.

Jefferson wasn't the only slaveholder in Philadelphia

for the momentous meeting of the Second Continental Congress that summer. In fact, the majority of the fifty-six men who signed the Declaration of Independence enslaved Black men, women, and children at the time. Some of the men enslaved several servants to work in their homes; others enslaved hundreds of people to work their plantations, (now called labor camps by some), build their houses, cook for their families, and take care of their personal needs. Two of the more famous delegates in attendance were Benjamin Franklin of Pennsylvania and John Hancock of Massachusetts, both now known as Founding Fathers. They each enslaved several people. John Adams, also from Massachusetts, was there for the signing, too. Adams, who would become the second president of the United States, was one of the only Founders to never enslave Africans.

HISTORY RECAP

The **Declaration of Independence** was written to permanently break ties with Great Britain. Though war had broken out a year earlier with the Battles of Lexington and Concord, the document officially declared war against the British Empire and explained why it was necessary. It was also created to persuade colonists who weren't so sure they wanted to break from Great Britain to back the cause for independence. And it was meant to help the colonies request aid from foreign governments.

The Declaration was adopted by the **Second Continental Congress**, meeting in Philadelphia, that was made up of delegates (representatives) from all thirteen colonies. Think of it as the United States' earliest form of national government. The First Continental Congress took place in 1774; the Second Continental Congress operated from 1775–1781.

Some of the most important men in this period of US history were not Declaration signers, but they're generally referred to as Founding Fathers for their critical roles in the formation of the United States. Included in this group are Alexander Hamilton, future secretary of the Treasury of the United States; James Madison, future fourth president of the United States; and, of course, George Washington, commander of the Continental Army fighting the British, and the future first president of the United States. These men enslaved people as well, although the story of Hamilton is a bit more complicated. (More about Hamilton in Chapter 3.)

The hypocrisy of the signers continuing to enslave people as they demanded their own freedom from British tyranny is not a new idea.

IT'S JUST A NAME, ISN'T IT?

In an exclusive interview with True History, Margaret Kimberley, senior columnist for *Black Agenda Report*, says the term **Founding Fathers** itself is problematic because it affirms patriarchy and white supremacy, and it has been elevated over time.

Patriarchy means a society or system of government run by men that gives women little or no power. *White supremacy* is the belief that white people are a superior race, which creates a structure of white domination over people of color and other cultures.

Kimberley says these men were not gods, though we often treat them as if they were. "People always talk about the Founders, the Founding Fathers, and they're deified [worshipped as a god] so you can't change anything in the Constitution . . . It keeps the country frozen in time, frozen in this moment of conquest, in enslavement. By deifying them, you deify what they did."

In this book, they are referred to simply as Founders and mostly leave *Fathers* behind.

Your teachers may have talked to you about viewing the lives of the men who shaped the nation in the context of the historical period. If we look at them through that lens, they certainly weren't the only slaveholders in 1776. That same year, enslaved Africans comprised around 20 percent of the population of the thirteen colonies and as much as 40 percent of the southern colonies. Slavery was permissible by law and was common, even in the northern colonies. It was a key to wealth and power, particularly in the South. And the Founders were men of wealth and power. They were elite patriarchs of a society governed by the belief in white supremacy.

Even as early as 1776, there were colonists advocating for the emancipation of enslaved people. For example, the Quakers, a religious group, opposed slavery. And just one year later, in 1777, Vermont became the first colony to ban slavery. But don't be fooled. This wasn't a very common point of view.

WHAT'S THAT WORD?

Emancipation is the process of setting free people who are enslaved. President Abraham Lincoln issued the

Emancipation Proclamation in 1863, declaring all people enslaved in the United States to be free. That was nearly one hundred years after the Declaration of Independence was written.

In this context, it might not be surprising that so many of these men owned slaves. What might be more surprising is to consider what some of those men actually thought of slavery. What did they believe should happen to the men, women, and children they enslaved? Did they think they should be freed? And how did their writings, public statements, and actions contradict the very words they wrote: "We hold these truths to be self-evident, that all men are created equal, that they are endowed by their Creator with certain unalienable rights, that among these are life, liberty and the pursuit of happiness."

And what did each Founder do, or fail to do, to end slavery?

II. A Declaration for Some

Leading up to the signing of the Declaration of Independence, some of the Founders wrote or spoke about the horrors of the slave trade. So why then didn't they include a plan to end slavery in the document?

In a testament to the power of editing, Jefferson wrote a clause attacking Great Britain's King George III that was ultimately left out of the Declaration of Independence. If it had been included, the country's relationship with slavery might have ended sooner—although that is up for debate.

> [H]e has waged cruel war against human nature itself, violating it's [sic] most sacred rights of life & liberty in the persons of a distant people who never offended him, captivating & carrying them into slavery in another hemisphere, or to incur miserable death in their transportation thither. [T]his piratical warfare, the opprobrium of infidel powers, is the warfare of the CHRISTIAN king of Great Britain. [D]etermined to keep open a market where MEN should be bought & sold, he has prostituted his negative for suppressing every legislative attempt to prohibit or restrain this execrable commerce: and that this assemblage of horrors might want no fact of distinguished die, he is now exciting those very people to rise in arms among us, and to purchase that liberty of which he has deprived them, & murdering the people upon whom he has obtruded them; thus paying off former crimes committed again the liberties of one people, with crimes which he urges them to commit against the lives of another.

Clearly, there's a lot to unpack here. *Opprobrium? Execrable commerce? Obtruded?* Let's look past the old-school language and break it all down from a modern perspective.

In the final version of the Declaration of Independence,

there are twenty-seven grievances—or complaints—specifically against Great Britain's King George III. These are all the reasons the Patriots wanted to be free of British rule.

HISTORY RECAP

The colonists wanted to be able to write their own laws and create their own representative government. The king was tightening his control over all aspects of the colonies: their rights, their economies, and their legal systems. They wanted to be free of those controls, what they called the *tyranny* (cruel and oppressive government rule) of the king. The last five grievances attack King George III for waging war on them.

Jefferson's omitted grievance has two important parts: The first accuses the king of inflicting the evil of slavery on the colonists and keeping it alive through the slave trade, as if against the colonists' will. Fact check: That was false. Nobody was forcing colonists to enslave people. The truth is, like so many other plantation owners, Jefferson was dependent on slavery. In fact, America's growing economy relied on the institution of slavery.

WHAT'S THE (RIGHT) WORD?

It's easy to use the word *slave*. But in recent years, the language used to talk and write about slavery has changed. Now, the preferred language is one of the following terms: ***enslaved person, a person who was enslaved, an African who was enslaved***, or ***an enslaved African***. Why? When you call someone a slave, you reduce them to an object. When you call someone a *person who was enslaved*, you recognize them as human first: a person with a family, history, intellect, and feelings.

Labor camp owners needed enslaved people to produce cotton, tobacco, wheat, and other crops and to sustain their enormous properties. In the North, some businessmen also relied on slavery, especially those in the shipping industry who made money trafficking Africans—forcing them onto ships to America to be bought and sold as property. So much of the young nation had been built by the labor of enslaved Africans. They built Jefferson's home, Monticello, and Washington's home, Mount Vernon. Later, the White House itself was primarily built by enslaved people.

The second part of Jefferson's grievance that needs some

unpacking is at the end of the passage. Here, Jefferson refers to the British proclamation of 1775 by Virginia governor Lord Dunmore. That proclamation offered freedom to enslaved people in the colonies if they signed up to fight for the British and were "able and willing to bear arms" against the Patriots. In the grievance, Jefferson is saying that through that proclamation, the king encouraged enslaved people to rise up against the colonists and murder them in order to win freedom. Of course, that proclamation was unsettling to colonists, particularly southerners who were already worried about revolts by enslaved people.

George Washington once called Lord Dunmore "that arch-traitor to the rights of humanity" for promising to free enslaved Africans who would fight for the Loyalists. But as you can imagine, that proclamation was effective: It enticed Black people to volunteer for the British cause, and it inspired thousands to try to escape to freedom behind British lines throughout the war.

Jefferson's grievance in the early draft of the Declaration sparked a heated debate among the delegates to the Continental Congress. Many of the delegates had no interest in ending slavery or including the passage in the country's mission statement, as slavery was a major source of their wealth and power. According to Jefferson's autobiography, the grievance was edited out to comply with the wishes of delegates from South Carolina and Georgia who wanted the slave trade to continue. He also believed that northern delegates were sympathetic to their southern colleagues because they represented businessmen involved in the Trans-Atlantic slave trade.

Whoever was responsible, there would ultimately be no mention of slavery in the final version of the Declaration of Independence. It's as if it didn't exist in the colonies at all. In reality, the young nation's roots in slavery ran deep and wide, and it would take many generations and another war to rip the institution out of the country's foundation.

REMEMBER THEIR NAMES

Black people weren't the only ones left out of the document. Women? There is no mention of white or Black women. They were neither considered equal to men nor consulted as politicians or writers. Women were locked out of the democratic process and would be for generations to come. But there was one white woman's name present on the Declaration of Independence: **Mary Katharine Goddard**.

Her name appears at the bottom: "Baltimore, in Maryland: Printed by Mary Katharine Goddard." In 1774, Goddard took control of *The Maryland Journal* as sole publisher, and during the Revolutionary War, her press shop issued the first edition of the Declaration in the colonies to include the signers' names. Staunchly opposed to British rule, Goddard was progressive and determined to use her paper to help reform the colonies. Goddard was appointed Maryland's postmaster, making her likely the US government's first female employee.

III. Propaganda

While Black people and women are not mentioned in the Declaration of Independence, Native Americans are. But not in a good way. The last grievance against King George III, number twenty-seven in the Declaration, doesn't get much attention. But it should.

> He has excited domestic insurrections amongst us, and has endeavoured to bring on the inhabitants of our frontiers, the merciless Indian Savages whose known rule of warfare, is an undistinguished destruction of all ages, sexes and conditions.

Professor Jeffrey Ostler, who teaches history at the University of Oregon, says the first part is again a reference to Lord Dunmore's Proclamation of 1775 offering freedom to enslaved people who fought for the British.

As for the phrase about the British unleashing the "merciless Indian savages" on colonial frontiersmen, it was propaganda. (*Propaganda* is information, often misleading or false, used to promote a political cause.) Ostler thinks Jefferson was trying to get the people on the frontier on board with the cause for independence by capitalizing on a common prejudice of Indigenous people.

Why? Land and money. The Proclamation of 1763

was issued by Britain's King George III at the end of the French and Indian War. That proclamation set a boundary line that restricted white settlement west of the Appalachian Mountains. This was a problem for land speculators—people like Jefferson and Washington—who were investing in land in those territories. Land speculators wanted their investments protected. They wanted to buy or steal land from Indigenous people, remove them, and sell the land to colonists. But they could only do that if they could secure titles to those lands. And the British had put up a roadblock with the proclamation.

WHAT'S THE (RIGHT) WORD?

Native American or Indigenous people? You may have heard either or both of these terms used and, depending on who you ask, they are both correct. In this book, we have chosen to use them interchangeably, just like the federal, state, and tribal governments do.

Ostler says Jefferson had a plan: "I think that the immediate play is to frontiers people who were (maybe a little bit more than people realize) rather ambivalent about the revolution. Some were supportive; many were not. They weren't sure independence would work, for one thing, and feared the coming of war."

But they also feared Indigenous people. And Jefferson knew it. It was something most settlers could rally around, so he played to those fears.

Ostler explains that the colonists weren't just fighting the British in the Revolutionary War. "There's a war within the war, and it's a war on the part of the colonists to subjugate Indigenous people to take their lands."

You were probably taught that the Revolutionary War was inspired by the Boston Tea Party and the Boston Massacre.

WHAT DOES *THAT* MEAN?

Settler colonialism is a form of colonialism in which an invading settler society seeks to replace the **Indigenous** (original) population of a territory (in this case the Native Americans), often through violence and domination.

Remember the political slogan, "No taxation without representation"? That's not incorrect. But Ostler says there is more to the story. He says that another of the motivating forces of the war was to acquire Native Americans' lands for colonial settlements and to kill or relocate the Indigenous population. This is known as settler colonialism, and it had the effect of helping to unify people. A common enemy often does that.

"I think in that experience of bloodshed, not only bloodshed at the hands of British forces, but bloodshed as they're fighting with Native Americans, there's a kind of forging of American nationalism that involves the bringing together of a people who have not really been a people," says Ostler. "I think that fighting of Indigenous people and the sense of them as an enemy, the 'merciless Indian savages' of Jefferson, now become a foe for the entire nation."

In other words, the newly created country was really still a sct of thirteen colonies that weren't united. There wasn't yet any consistent sense of American pride in the colonies. Having common enemies, the British and the Indigenous people, helped to bring together those colonies and their citizens, with the common goal to defeat them.

HISTORY RECAP

Throughout US history, politicians have often played on white Americans' fears as a way of consolidating power. We've witnessed this through attempts to instill fear of Black people during the civil rights movement, fear of Latino immigrants, and fear of Muslims and Black Lives Matter protestors during the Trump Administration.

Can you think of other times in history when politicians used fear of a so-called enemy for political gain?

IV. Living Up to Those Founding Ideals

You may have heard about the *New York Times'* "1619 Project," and you may have even read some of it. The project is a series of essays and articles that seek to reframe US history by putting the legacy of slavery and the many contributions of Black Americans at the center of the United States' story. It's called the "1619 Project" because that was the year that a ship arrived in Point Comfort in the colony of Virginia, carrying the first twenty or more enslaved people from Africa to British North America.

The creator of the project is *New York Times* journalist Nikole Hannah-Jones. In her lead essay, she writes that enslaved Black people—who had been taken from their homes in Africa and enslaved by colonists for more than 150 years by the time the Declaration of Independence was written—were completely left out of its process, the product, and its promise. Like Jefferson's body servant, Robert Hemings, they were not free to pursue their dreams.

"'Life, Liberty and the pursuit of Happiness' did not apply to fully one-fifth of the country," Hannah-Jones writes. And she draws a connection from the founding of the country to the United States of the twenty-first century: "Yet despite being violently denied the freedom and justice promised to all, black Americans believed fervently in the American creed. Through centuries of black resistance and protest, we have helped the country live up to its founding ideals. And not only for ourselves—black rights struggles paved the way for every other rights struggle, including women's and gay rights, immigrant and disability rights."

All those struggles continue in different forms today. The legacy of slavery still impacts daily life in the United States, where systemic anti-Black racism infects multiple aspects of US society. Systemic racism keeps a disproportionate number of Black men imprisoned and makes them more vulnerable to arrest and police violence. It also hurts some Black Americans economically, as it limits opportunities for success in some primarily Black communities.

The genocide and displacement of Indigenous people still shape their lives today. These communities struggle to reclaim land and economic security after a long, painful history. That history has negatively affected generations of Indigenous people.

Some people believe that going back and taking a more critical look at the founding of the United States undermines the American story and divides us as a nation. But Linnea Grim, vice president of guest experiences at Jefferson's home, Monticello, offers another perspective in an interview with True History.

Reexamining the founders, you reexamine the flaws so you can form a more perfect union and be able to achieve the words of the Declaration. You learn from the mistakes of the past. Jefferson, Adams, all of them—that's what they were doing when they were looking back at history. They were voracious readers of history as they were shaping the document. . . . You look back, and you see what worked well and what didn't, and really try to understand it to make a better present and future.

It can be difficult to understand why events that happened so long ago, and people who lived so long ago, matter now. But the more we know—the more you know—about this history, the more we can begin to understand why the United States has the problems of racial inequality that we see today. There are direct links from past to present. And some of those links continue to harm some US citizens. If Americans can better understand those links, they can begin to break those that continue to do damage to the country. Then it may become possible to better unite the people of the United States so that every person enjoys the full meaning of Jefferson's words.

LET'S TALK ABOUT IT

* Nikole Hannah-Jones writes in the "1619 Project" that "[t]he United States is a nation founded on both an ideal and a lie." What do you think she means by that?

CHAPTER 2
A COMPLICATED LEGACY:
THOMAS JEFFERSON

On a Friday evening in August 2017, a crowd of several hundred protestors, including leaders of white supremacy groups, gathered in Charlottesville, Virginia, for the opening night of what they called the Unite the Right rally. They came together with a purpose: to promote the US white nationalist movement and to oppose the removal of a statue of Confederate General Robert E. Lee from a park. Some protestors carried tiki torches and weapons. Some waved Confederate and neo-Nazi flags. Others wore tactical vests and Nazi armbands. They chanted neo-Nazi and white supremacist slogans. Together, the protestors marched toward another statue: that of Thomas Jefferson, on the campus of the University of Virginia.

Was it coincidence they had chosen a school founded by Thomas Jefferson, nearly two hundred years earlier, and his likeness? Or did they head there on purpose?

HISTORY RECAP

The Confederacy was the breakaway Southern states that fought against the United States during the Civil War, from 1861 to 1865. Most Americans consider Confederate statues and the Confederate flag offensive today because they represent a long history of slavery, oppression, and segregation.

There are many Americans who want to tear down Confederate statues like those of General Robert E. Lee, and some people who want to remove statues of Presidents Jefferson and Washington because of their relationship to slavery. Others believe all these statues represent important pieces of US history and should remain standing.

Historian and Jefferson biographer Annette Gordon-Reed notes a difference between statues of Lee and Jefferson. "I would draw a clear line between the Confederates and the Confederacy and members of the founding generation. I think there's every difference between people who helped to create the United States versus people who tried to destroy the United States."

Chapter 1 discussed that *white supremacists* believe white people are a superior race and support a structure of white domination over people of color and other cultures. *White nationalists* hold supremacist views and believe that whites should have their own country. The two terms have a lot in common, but they're not exactly the same.

Anti-Semitism is discrimination against and/or hostility toward Jewish people. Anti-Semitism is often a key component of white supremacists' beliefs.

There is a long-standing tradition in American culture, politics, and education to look back on the early days of the nation with great reverence but through a faulty, selective memory. What does that mean? It means that people tend to remember the past the way they want to remember it, often forgetting all the bad events that happened, especially if they didn't affect them personally. It's the way US history often teaches the heroic aspects of the country's founding, glossing over the more brutal and less appealing parts, like colonization and the legacy of slavery. Hasan Kwame Jeffries, associate history professor at The Ohio State University, calls this "hard history." He says that Americans hate history but love nostalgia: "Nostalgia is the opposite of that hard history. Nostalgia is the stories about the past that make us feel good about the present. So we want to know about George Washington cutting down cherry trees. But we don't want to hear about him chasing down Ona Judge. [See Chapter 6.] The nostalgia makes us feel good. This is our origin story. This is our myth. This is who we are as a people. But it's not real. That's the Disney version of the past."

In a similar tradition, many Americans remember previous decades, like the 1950s, for example, as a simpler, better, and easier way of life. They are nostalgic for that time.

Why? In the 1950s, the average (white) man could make a decent living, buy a home, and support his family, often without going to college—and achieve the American dream. It was financially easier for many families than it is now. That is the 1950s American way of life many older people remember today. But they forget about the way life was for marginalized groups, including women, Black Americans, and the LGBTQ community in the 1950s. They forget that *hard history*.

WHAT DOES *THAT* MEAN?

The American dream is an abstract idea with different meanings depending on whom you ask. Most agree it means that though hard work, every American has the opportunity to succeed. In America, success has traditionally been defined by money and home ownership.

Most Americans don't have enough money saved to pay for a house in full. So they apply for a loan from a bank called a mortgage. Here's where the rules become uneven between minorities and white people.

Beginning in 1934, some government officials did not want people who lived in poorer, minority neighborhoods to be able to purchase a home, so they came up with a plan called redlining. The officials literally drew red lines on the maps for banks to know in which zip codes to turn down mortgage requests, denying those individuals a shot at the American dream. This continued until the Fair Housing Act of 1968, but the effects of redlining are still felt in minority communities today.

This is just one example of systemic racism, discussed in Chapter 1.

With each new generation of Americans, there is a renewed tug-of-war between the desire to move forward and the competing desire to return to the past, that "simpler time." That instinct to go backward is likely based on fear of the unknown (the future); a distaste for a faster pace of life (technological advances); or simply a nostalgia for the past. But sometimes, this desire comes from a place of prejudice, a longing for a time when white Christian people, men in particular, held tighter controls over all aspects of a more segregated US society. It can also be motivated by a fear that white people will eventually be the minority in the United States.

When pushed to the extreme, this desire to return to that past can be dangerous, even deadly. Unfortunately, extreme white supremacist views have been on the rise in the United States and in other parts of the world.

On day two of the Unite the Right rally in Charlottesville, extremist protestors—armed with weapons, bigotry, and symbols of hatred—clashed with counterprotestors. As tensions rose between the two groups, an American terrorist rammed his car into a crowd, injuring dozens and killing a young counterprotestor named Heather Heyer.

What does all this have to do with Thomas Jefferson, you ask?

Today, most Americans remember Jefferson as an eloquent author, revered Founder, and the third president of the United States. It's undeniable that he had a major impact on the founding of the United States and its expansion. Among his accomplishments, his words in the Declaration of Independence have resonated for generations because of their elegance and promise.

But it's not surprising that those protestors—many of whom were white nationalists and white supremacists—chose a school founded by Jefferson, and his statue, as one of their meeting places. Jefferson was a lifelong slaveholder who held what we now call white supremacist and white nationalist beliefs. And while Jefferson deserves to be remembered and praised for his positive accomplishments in shaping the United States, there is more to his story than you might have been told. It is through Jefferson, possibly more than any other American, as Gordon-Reed says, that you can have discussions about race, slavery, politics, and gender.

So much of Jefferson's story is encapsulated in his home, Monticello.

II. Shadow Plantation

Located near Charlottesville, Virginia, at the edge of the Blue Ridge Mountains, is Monticello, or "little mountain" in Italian. Linnea Grim, the vice president of guest experiences at Monticello, now a National Historic Landmark, says it's more like a hill to visitors from mountainous regions.

Jefferson inherited the land from his father and began building on that hill in 1769, when he was twenty-six. He was a self-taught architect, so he designed the home himself. But it was enslaved Black people who did most of the hard labor, just as they built so much of the country's roads, railways, and buildings.

Grim says Monticello reflects Jefferson's thinking for both good and ill. It also reflects the state of the nation in the late eighteenth century. "Monticello is a microcosm of the strengths and flaws of the US at the time," says Grim. "You see what many people would say are good American characteristics such as ingenuity, not being trapped by tradition, . . . the ability to use science and reason, and you see that everywhere throughout the property. And then, of course, you see slavery."

Jefferson's impressive mansion on the hill must have

wowed eighteenth-century guests arriving at the plantation for the first time. The house and property are grand and vast, and Jefferson lived a life of luxury.

The people Jefferson enslaved lived a very different kind of life.

Monticello's main house sits atop a long tunnel, with an icehouse at one end and a kitchen at the other, where the enslaved worked tirelessly to feed Jefferson, his family, and frequent guests. Behind the house was the shabby Mulberry Row, the main plantation street at Monticello and its industrial center, which included crude cabins where some of the enslaved lived, workshops, and storehouses. It was what Jeffries called a slave-labor camp.

Slavery was the economic engine for the entire South. And it was profitable for Jefferson as well. In addition to the tobacco and wheat crops the enslaved laborers planted and harvested, Jefferson exploited the talents of his enslaved artisans, carpenters, and masons to produce goods—things like nails, barrels, and textiles. And it was the enslaved people themselves who were valuable. Every time a woman Jefferson enslaved gave birth, that meant he enslaved an additional human being who would grow to be a valuable worker, raised in bondage.

In his own words: "I consider a woman who brings a child every two years as more profitable than the best man of the farm."

Jefferson trained children for some jobs, and the work could be grueling. For three years, Jefferson himself oversaw the nailery, where boys ages ten to sixteen toiled daily. He used incentives, like money and clothing, to push the boys to work harder.

WHAT'S THAT WORD?

In bondage is the state of being enslaved and forced to work for one's enslaver.

Violence was also an incentive at Monticello. Although there is no record of Jefferson himself physically hurting anyone, the overseers he hired did beat people. A few of his overseers had reputations for being particularly cruel.

At any given time, there were as many as two hundred enslaved people at Monticello and Jefferson's other properties. In Jefferson's lifetime, he owned over six hundred enslaved people, which even by eighteenth-century standards was a lot. Jefferson inherited enslaved people from his father and even more from his father-in-law. He purchased additional people, and still others were born into bondage at Monticello.

Despite what we now know about Jefferson, he considered himself a benevolent (good) slaveholder.

Gordon-Reed says, "Now, we balk at that—and rightfully so—but he saw himself as doing slavery in the right way, if it had to be done." She adds that because he viewed himself as a good slaveholder, there was less urgency to end slavery.

Being a nice or decent slaveholder is, of course, a contradiction in itself. It is impossible to be a good slaveholder. And the conscious act of being kind to the people who labored for him suggests that Jefferson saw their humanity—in other words, he recognized that they were human beings. Like so many of the other Founders, he understood the institution of slavery to be immoral and unjust. He denounced slavery in public while in private exploiting the institution for profit, political gain, and power. All the Founders left the issue of slavery to future generations to figure out.

While it is clear that Jefferson was a born-and-bred slaveholder, he still grappled with the very institution and the ethics of slavery. Jefferson writes in *Notes on the State of*

Virginia, "The whole commerce between master and slave is a perpetual exercise of the most boisterous passions, the most unremitting despotism on the one part, and degrading submissions on the other."

In his only full-length work, published in 1785, Jefferson acknowledges that the system of slavery turned enslavers into cruel dictators who ruled with absolute power while humiliating the enslaved, who held no power. In short, he recognizes in writing that the institution of slavery is wrong and disgusting. But he continued to hold racist views about Black people.

He continues in *Notes*, writing that Black people were "inferior to the whites in the endowments of both mind and body." Despite these overtly racist musings, Jefferson seems to understand that the conditions of their bondage had hurt enslaved people (beyond the physical)—namely, having had no education. And yet he still calls them inferior, not only to whites, but to Native Americans as well.

III. The Jefferson Paradox

When Jefferson was elected to serve as the third president of the United States in 1800, he envisioned a country that stretched from "sea to shining sea." He saw each new colony being equal to the thirteen original colonies of the union, writes historian Stephen Ambrose. With the Louisiana Purchase of 1803, President Jefferson doubled the size of the country. It was another opportunity to free enslaved Africans or initiate a policy of gradual emancipation. And yet, slavery would continue for another sixty-two years.

Ironically, while Haiti became an independent country run by newly freed people as a result of the revolution, the Louisiana Purchase increased the number of enslaved people in the United States. And it led to a policy to forcibly remove Indigenous people from the territory.

The original treaty stated that "inhabitants of the ceded territory" would have the same rights as all US citizens. But Jefferson revised it to read "white inhabitants," excluding not only Black people but the Indigenous people who already lived there. Again, an incredibly significant edit and omission, like that grievance left out of the Declaration of Independence.

"Had Jefferson wanted to end the evil of slavery he could have done it with the stroke of a pen," Margaret Kimberley writes in her book, *Prejudential: Black America and the Presidents.*

HISTORY RECAP

The **Louisiana Purchase** was a treaty: a land deal between the United States and France. For $15 million, the United States bought approximately 828,000 square miles of land west of the Mississippi. France only actually controlled a small portion of the land; most of it was inhabited by Native Americans. And the driving force behind the sale was the Haitian Revolution.

The **Haitian Revolution** of 1791–1804 was the most successful slave rebellion in history. Enslaved persons on the island of Haiti rose up against French colonial rule, and after years of bloody battles, the insurrection was victorious, and slavery there ended. French leader Napoleon Bonaparte had planned to set up a French presence in the Louisiana Territory, but without goods like sugar coming from Haiti, and without the slave labor from the island, there would be nothing to trade. The French were shaken by the Haitian Revolution and realized that the dream of a French empire in the Americas was not viable. Jefferson was all too happy to keep the French away from the United States, and the deal was struck.

Gordon-Reed says Jefferson's inaction around slavery was partly driven by his political ambition. If Jefferson had announced that he was going to end slavery, it would have sunk his political future. "I don't think he would have been vice president. I don't think he would have been president."

Even if he had decided to free enslaved populations, Jefferson believed they should be removed from the United States and sent to live in Africa or the West Indies. Why? Because he thought they could never live peacefully with their former slaveholders and would start a race war. And Jefferson knew whites wouldn't let go of their prejudices.

In a 2019 interview with Walter Isaacson on PBS, Gordon-Reed said the marchers in Charlottesville chose Jefferson's statue because of this white nationalist belief that Black Americans could not live in harmony with white people and therefore must be separated. Gordon-Reed notes Jefferson tended to be an optimist but not on this subject. "The people marching towards the statue, I think, were doing so as a way of claiming him for that kind of ideal."

But she also points out that the marchers were met by counterprotestors at the statue who held opposing beliefs. "Now there were people surrounding the statue, who, whether they liked Jefferson or not, were standing for the other ideals of Jefferson . . . ideals of the Declaration, actually—the notion of all men are created equal, pursuit of happiness, the American creed. So you had this clash, the American clash that we've had from the very, very beginning: Are we one people? Embodied in that particular moment."

That clash of ideals between those who want to live in a united country where all races and religions are welcome and treated equally and those who see the United States as a primarily white, Christian nation is still alive today.

IV. A Tragic Legacy

Throughout his life, Jefferson would come out in favor of the gradual emancipation of Black people, but he often didn't practice what he preached. He famously wrote that maintaining slavery was like holding "the wolf by the ear, and we can neither hold him, nor safely let him go." He feared if freed Black people would rise up and seek revenge against their former enslavers.

He also said that if enslaved people were free, they wouldn't be able to take care of themselves. In a 1788 letter, he wrote, "to abandon persons whose habits have been formed in slavery is like abandoning children."

In 1807, toward the end of his second term in office, President Jefferson did eventually sign a law prohibiting the importation of enslaved persons into the United States from Africa and elsewhere. But the new law did not stop people from keeping the enslaved people they already owned, or their future children, in bondage.

Jefferson may have believed that slavery was evil and that it would eventually disappear. But in helping create and expand a settler colonial state built on Indigenous lands, using the wealth generated by slavery, it wasn't to his advantage to end it. He profited from slavery. He profited from the country's system of white supremacy that he helped preserve and protect, from the labor of the people he enslaved, and from the very existence of those people.

Slavery would not be outlawed in the United States until 1865, when the Thirteenth Amendment was added to the Constitution, and after a four-year Civil War that left an estimated 750,000 Americans dead.

Jeffries says, "When slavery ends, white supremacy doesn't. So the beliefs that undergird slavery, that allow for people to be held in bondage, that allow for this dehumanization, do not end when slavery ends. They carry forward. And that's part of that legacy because that then serves as a justification/rationalization for the continued racial discrimination in America."

And that's one of the reasons we have to look more critically at the past: to see the lines that connect the origin story of the United States with the present. Jeffries says we have to figure out how to disrupt those lines to end racial discrimination. If we ignore or avoid hard history, we cannot successfully break those links.

Fifty years after he signed the Declaration of Independence, Jefferson died on July 4, 1826. (John Adams died the same day.) He had lived a lavish life at Monticello, beyond his means, and he was in debt: around $100,000, the equivalent of $2 million today.

The result was a nightmare for the people he enslaved. To pay his debtors, Jefferson's family had to sell his property, which included humans. Many were related to one another and had lived together as families for years at Monticello. In total, 133 people were sold at two auctions, tearing apart families and friends and sending them to different parts of the country. Six months after his death, there was an auction to sell off the personal estate of Thomas Jefferson.

Jefferson officially freed only two people in his lifetime: Robert Hemings, the body servant discussed in Chapter 1, and Robert's brother James. He freed five people in his will; two of them were children he fathered with a woman named Sally Hemings. Her story is next.

LET'S TALK ABOUT IT

* Do you think Jefferson could have done more to end slavery?
* What does the American Dream mean to you?

CHAPTER 3
AN AMERICAN LIFE:
SALLY HEMINGS

If you Google Sally Hemings's image, you'll find a painting of a pretty, young Black woman with a light complexion, long dark hair, and other features that correspond to modern white ideals of beauty. She looks thoughtful and serene—someone in control of her life. It appears to be an actual portrait of Hemings. But there is no historical, visual record of what Hemings looked like, and that portrait—which is often the first image that pops up in an internet search—was conjured from the imagination of an artist. Like most enslaved people, Hemings never sat for a portrait. But that painting is how many people picture her now.

When Monticello decided to add an exhibit dedicated to Sally Hemings, the staff created a moving audio-visual presentation of the woman Jefferson enslaved, the mother to at least six of his children. It purposefully acknowledges what historians know about Hemings and what they don't.

"There was a long conversation about how to represent Hemings, because we didn't know what she looked like. We decided on a silhouette shape and casting shadows on the walls, rather than making something up," says Linnea Grim.

The Hemings exhibit is located in a room where she might have lived at Monticello, with shadows projected onto walls as the words of her son Madison tell her story.

More is known about her life than her appearance. But it's not through her own words; it's through her son's recounting and the words of others. Grim says there are so many missing pieces in the histories of enslaved people.

"One of the tragedies of slavery is the erasure of the record of human personalities," says Grim. "When you have the written record, you get to see so much more of a person. Slavery erased so much because those people who controlled the system didn't think other humans, or their stories, were of value."

Sally Hemings gets her own chapter in this book because although Jefferson omitted her from the written record of his life, she was an integral part of it and deserves her own pages. Grim says it's important to tell her story.

> In looking at American history, her name is often an attachment point to Jefferson's name, but we're now seeing Hemings's story as a quintessential American story. Her story is as American, if not more American, than Jefferson's story because of what her life encompassed, the challenges she had, what her descendants were able to achieve in the face of systemic racism that many of them still face, that is the American story. Talking about the life of Sally Hemings is talking about an American life.

The history of that life is complicated. The short version is this: Heming's mother, Elizabeth (Betty) Hemings, was considered the property of John Wayles of Charles City County, Virginia. One of John Wayles's children was Martha, who would become Jefferson's wife. When Wayles's third wife died, John took Betty as his enslaved "concubine." He fathered six of her children, including Sally. These children were the half siblings of Martha, but they remained enslaved.

Shortly after Martha Wayles married Thomas Jefferson, her father died. The couple inherited all her father's enslaved persons, which included the Hemings family, who came to live at Monticello.

WHAT'S THAT WORD?

Concubine is a mistress to a man who either has a wife or cannot marry the woman because of her lower social status. A concubine usually lives with or close to a man who is dominant over her, and she often has children with him. Within the context of slavery, "concubines" did not have a choice in whether or not to participate.

* * *

II. Hemings in Paris

Just a heads-up: There is some material in this section that some readers may find particularly disturbing.

The Jeffersons had two daughters, Martha and Mary. Sally Hemings was close in age to Martha and about three years older than Mary. Hemings acted as nursemaid and companion, a chambermaid, and a seamstress. When Martha senior died, Jefferson went to Paris to be the American foreign minister to France (an ambassador). He brought his daughter Martha and left Mary behind. But soon he called for Mary to join them and ordered Sally Hemings—who was fourteen years old—to accompany the girl as her body servant.

(Remember: Her brother Robert was Jefferson's body servant for a long time.)

It is impossible to know what it must have been like for young Sally to move that far away from her family, to travel across the ocean to live at the Hôtel de Langeac in Paris. There are no letters, diary entries, or other written records to indicate how she felt. Those holes in the historical record raise so many questions: Was she scared? Was she excited to see a new city? Was she aware before she left Virginia that she would be considered a free woman in France?

And there are many questions around what happened between Hemings and Jefferson. There's little record of that beyond her son Madison's account. He called his mother Jefferson's "concubine." (There is no record of how Jefferson's daughters felt about their father's activities, either. Surely, they must have had opinions about it.)

It is known that Jefferson had Hemings vaccinated for smallpox at great expense. And he took her shopping in Paris for clothing, which was quite unusual. Normally, an enslaved woman would have made her own clothing.

In her book *The Hemingses of Monticello*, historian Annette Gordon-Reed says Jefferson saw himself as a patriarchal figure. Gordon-Reed explains that Hemings had never known her father. Her mother and siblings, except for her older brother James, who was also in Paris, were back in Virginia. And she was in a new country with a different language. Jefferson was in charge of her life in that strange place.

By modern standards, when evaluating what transpired between these two people, we look at the power dynamic at play and the history of rape perpetrated by white masters against the Black women they enslaved. On a more personal level, we can't help but wonder about the switch in Hemings's mind from viewing Jefferson as the master of the house to something more sinister when he decided to start having sex with her. Her mother and her grandmother were both "concubines" of their enslavers, as Madison put it, so it would have been familiar to her. It is impossible to know what she thought.

By modern standards, Hemings was a child—a teen when Jefferson began to have sex with her, sometime between the ages of fourteen and sixteen. At the time in Virginia, the age of consent (the age at which a person is legally able to agree to sexual acts) was, remarkably, just ten. (In 2021, it was

A CLOSER LOOK

Across the South at that time, it was common for white men to rape the women they enslaved and father their children. It was something men didn't talk about (which is unsurprising), and there were no consequences for their brutality. It was taboo, but everyone knew it was happening.

Some historians are conflicted (many are not) over whether to call Jefferson's actions rape. But whatever you call it, Jefferson never spoke publicly about Hemings and didn't respond to a newspaper report that exposed him, nor the reports that followed. And that silence speaks volumes, says Grim.

"One of the things that I've wondered about over the years that I've worked at Monticello is what Jefferson thought about his connection with Sally Hemings. In all the extant documents that historians have, he never acknowledges his sexual relationship with Hemings or being the father of their children. The absence of any mention of her means he did not willingly share what he was doing with correspondents. This leads me to think that he considered what he was doing wrong. But my question is, What did he think he was doing wrong? I have a feeling that what many of us think he did wrong and what he thinks he did wrong are not the same thing."

eighteen in Virginia and as young as sixteen in some states.) But no matter what her age, consent didn't apply in this case because Sally was Jefferson's property. He had legal control over her body, and she would have been bound to do as he demanded.

Jefferson was thirty years older. But at that time, girls as young as Hemings would have been considered old enough to become seriously involved with men, even much older ones. There was no teenager designation in the eighteenth century, and once a girl hit puberty, she was considered a woman, sexually.

Grim says, "Age however still comes into play when you're talking about Hemings and Jefferson because there was such a huge age difference. . . . It's gut-wrenching for most people today to be thinking about that and acknowledging that it was a different conception of childhood and adulthood at that time."

Gordon-Reed says even though Hemings could not have consented or said no to him, there is no way to know how Jefferson approached Hemings or how he treated her in Paris. She says Jefferson was charming and wanted people to like him. And he tended to appeal to people's emotions by doing things for them to make them feel grateful and bound to him. In Hemings's case, the vaccine and the clothing could be seen as examples of this.

III. To Leave or Not to Leave

Slavery was illegal in France, and if a slaveholder brought his human property there from the colonies, he risked losing them to the protections of French law. Hemings knew this and entered into a kind of negotiation with Jefferson, according to her son Madison.

> Their stay (my mother's and Maria's) was about eighteen months. But during that time my mother became Mr. Jefferson's concubine, and when he was called back home she was enciente [pregnant] by him. He desired to bring my mother back to Virginia with him but she demurred [raised objections]. She was just beginning to understand the French language well, and in France she was free, while if she returned to Virginia she would be re-enslaved. So she refused to return with him. To induce her to do so he promised her extraordinary privileges, and made a solemn pledge that her children should be freed at the age of twenty-one years. In consequence of his promise, on which she implicitly relied, she returned with him to Virginia.

Gordon-Reed says at first it was a mystery to her why Hemings didn't stay in Paris so that she could be free. In a National Public Radio interview, Gordon-Reed said, "But when I started writing *The Hemingses of Monticello* and working on that, and I realized how important family was, I began to think about how important family would have been to someone like that, a sixteen-year-old female raised to believe that she had some special connection to family, in a way, to think about family, think about your mother is back in Virginia. Her sisters and brothers were there."

And her pregnancy would have complicated everything for Hemings. You can imagine that she wouldn't have wanted to raise her baby by herself, without her mother or other family members around her. Staying behind in a foreign country to raise her child alone would have been a frightening prospect.

Gordon-Reed says that Hemings might have believed Jefferson's promises because he treated the Hemings family better than other enslaved people. The Hemings women, for example, were the only enslaved women at Monticello who didn't have to work the fields at harvest time.

"I have a particular view of Jefferson from this particular time and seeing him as, for lack of a better term, an enemy of these people. But it's not clear to me that she would have seen it in exactly the same way that I did. And that's one of the things you have to do when you're writing history is whatever you would want people to do, they may not think about things in the same way."

So much about the Sally Hemings story asks us to consider the context of the time period. That can be difficult and frustrating because the subject matter is so disturbing. It also asks us to try to see the world through Hemings's eyes. Yet that is so difficult when we don't have her words to consider.

IV. Back on the Hill

Gordon-Reed says that the idea that a man would have a mistress—a woman who was not his wife—was normal in Virginia at that time. It would not have been unusual for a widowed white man to take one of his enslaved women as a substitute for a wife. (White people couldn't legally marry Black people until 1967 in Virginia.) And Jefferson had promised his wife, Martha, on her deathbed, that he would never remarry.

Gordon-Reed believes Jefferson developed an attachment to Hemings. She says we can't look at every Black-white, enslaved-enslaver relationship the same way. "I think there were different types of connections. And Jefferson, to me, shows signs of having been attached to Sally Hemings. I have no problem saying that because there are no stories about him with any other woman when he comes back from France, you know, ever but her. We don't know about her because once she gets back here, she is totally under his power."

Jefferson's attachment to Hemings lasted forty years, and he fathered six children with her; four lived to adulthood. Their names were Beverly, Harriet, Madison, and Eston—three boys and one girl.

In his memoir, Madison reflected on his childhood.

> We were permitted to stay about the "great house," and only required to do such light work as going on errands. Harriet learned to spin and to weave in a little factory on the home plantation. We were free from the dread of having to be slaves all our lives long, and were measurably happy. We were always permitted to be with our mother, who was well used. It was her duty, all her life which I can remember, up to the time of father's death, to take care of his chamber and wardrobe, look after us children and do such light work as sewing, and Provision was made in the will of our father that we should be free when we arrived at the age of 21 years.

Jefferson was against miscegenation—the mixing of different races—and believed that when freed, Black people must be "removed beyond the reach of mixture." And yet, he fathered six mixed-raced children with a mixed-race woman. Did he treat them like his kids? The short answer is no. They remained enslaved until adulthood. The two eldest children left Monticello as adults with Jefferson's permission and were able to pass for whites. The other two were later freed. And according to Madison Hemings, he did not act as a typical father.

> He was uniformly kind to all about him. He was not in the habit of showing partiality or fatherly affection to us children. We were the only children of his by a slave woman. He was affectionate toward his white grandchildren, of whom he had fourteen, twelve of whom lived to manhood and womanhood.

Notice that Madison makes the distinction between the way Jefferson treated him and his siblings and the way he treated his white daughters' children. To Jefferson, who did not believe that white and Black people should mix, his children's very existence would have been problematic for him and a constant reminder of the contradiction between his beliefs and practices.

Sally Hemings was never formally freed. But she was able to leave Monticello in 1826 with her two youngest sons, Madison and Eston, when they were emancipated upon Jefferson's death.

WHAT DOES *THAT* MEAN?

Passing for white is what it sounds like. There is a long history of mixed-race people who look white living as white people to avoid being enslaved or, later after slavery was outlawed, discriminated against. Sometimes in one family, as in the Hemings family, some children could pass for white while others could not. And sometimes that meant families separating—those passing as white having to deny their relationship to those in their family who looked Black. While the person passing as white may have gained opportunities, they may have also lost their senses of their heritage, their connections to family, and their communities.

V. Declaring Jefferson the Father

A journalist names James Callender reported on the relationship (for lack of a better word) between Jefferson and Hemings during Jefferson's first term in the White House. It was quite scandalous. Other newspapers also picked up the story. Even so, biographers, some Jefferson descendants, and other groups attached to him repeatedly denied the relationship and the paternity of Hemings's children for many years. The story did not fit the narrative of an admirable Founder, the third commander in chief, and the man who wrote the Declaration of Independence.

It took women to correct the record. The first was Fawn

M. Brodie, who wrote a biography in 1974. Following in Brodie's footsteps, Gordon-Reed's meticulous research led to a number of books, including *Thomas Jefferson and Sally Hemings: An American Controversy* published in 1997. In her book, Gordon-Reed lays out in great detail the case that the relationship existed and that Jefferson fathered six children with Hemings. She also details the prejudices of the deniers and how racism led to incorrect assessments of Jefferson and Hemings. For example, many people did not believe Madison Hemings because he was a Black man and formerly enslaved person.

Gordon-Reed's book ignited a renewed interest in the subject, and in 1998, a DNA test of descendants of the Jefferson line and the Eston Hemings line concluded there was a match. The combination of these results and other historical evidence led to the conclusion that Jefferson fathered Hemings's children. According to Monticello, it is a settled matter.

Through their books, Brodie and Gordon-Reed have corrected the record by detailing the lives of this family who was such an important part of life at Monticello. Linnea Grim notes one of the tragedies of slavery is not having a written record of people who were enslaved. It is through the Hemingses' and other enslaved Americans' stories that we can learn more about the history of Black Americans and the history of America itself. Yet, there is still so much we'd like to know about these individuals as humans. For example, what was Hemings truly like? Was she funny? What made her laugh? Or was she more serious?

Like so many stories stricken from the record, we'll never know. A very different kind of American life is up next.

LET'S TALK ABOUT IT

* Why do you think Sally Hemings decided to return to Virginia with Jefferson, even though it meant giving up her chance to be free?

* Linnea Grim says she thinks Jefferson knew he was doing something wrong in his relationship with Hemings. But that what he thought was wrong was probably different than what we think was wrong with it. What do you think Jefferson thought was wrong?

CHAPTER 4
ABOLITIONIST OR SLAVEHOLDER?: ALEXANDER HAMILTON

If you've seen *Hamilton*, either the film or the original cast of the Broadway show, you might picture Lin-Manuel Miranda when you read about Alexander Hamilton. The two are synonymous now, even though they look nothing alike. Hamilton was a white man with reddish hair and azure-blue eyes, while Miranda is of Puerto Rican descent with dark eyes and hair. But Miranda and Hamilton have something in common: a way with words. Hamilton was a gifted orator with an extraordinary ability to write quickly and persuasively. Miranda is the writer, actor, and star of *Hamilton*, and the man behind the ingenious lyrics and rapid-fire delivery showcased in the musical's forty-six songs. You can imagine a verbal duel between the two men ending in a draw and exhaustion, though less deadly than the gun duel with Aaron Burr that took Hamilton's life.

Miranda wrote his first Broadway hit, *In the Heights*, when he was still in college. And college is where Alexander Hamilton—future Founder, Treasury secretary of the United States and face of the ten-dollar bill—first made his mark as a courageous, revolutionary, and charismatic leader. Like the twenty-first-century activists integral to the anti-gun violence and climate change movements, Hamilton was young and outspoken.

In 1774, he was also in the right place at the right time, at Kings College (now Columbia University) in New York City. For many political leaders, pioneers, and titans of industry, time and place are often as critical to their success as talent and drive. Hamilton was no exception. But he wasn't born into a life of success.

Although Hamilton was endowed with verbal and literary gifts and ambition to match, he wasn't raised in the right place, or under the right circumstances, for the kind of success he was aiming for. In a stratified world (meaning one divided into economic and social classes), that could have been enough to quash his dreams. But after a tough childhood on the islands of Nevis and Saint Croix, he managed to find his way to New York, where the teen could be a new man, leave the past behind, and find acceptance with the social elite. Alexander Hamilton was, after all, a serious social climber.

WHERE'S THAT?

Nevis and Saint Croix

Nevis is a small Caribbean island in the West Indies. Nevis and Saint Kitts together form one country called the Federation of Saint Kitts and Nevis. **Saint Croix** is one of the US Virgin Islands, also in the Caribbean.

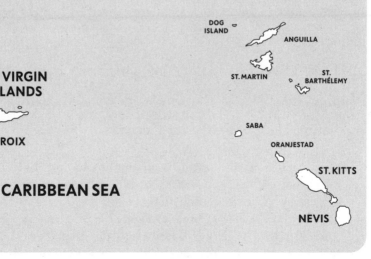

DOG ISLAND

ANGUILLA

ST. MARTIN

ST. BARTHÉLEMY

US VIRGIN ISLANDS

SABA

ST. CROIX

ORANJESTAD

ST. KITTS

CARIBBEAN SEA

NEVIS

II. A Rough Start

A young Alexander Hamilton was raised mostly on Saint Croix by his mother, Rachel Faucette, since he was abandoned by his father, James Hamilton. His childhood was marked by one tragedy after another. He and his older brother were left poor and parentless after their father disappeared, and their mother died in 1768. Shortly after that, their cousin, who was also their guardian, died by suicide. Just about everyone else in their family was dead by the time the brothers were fourteen and sixteen.

Hamilton needed cash and went to work for a mercantile house—an import/export business—called Beekman and Cruger. It was a good, respectable job. And lucky for him, he was taken in by a successful merchant, Thomas Stevens, and his wife.

Then tragedy struck again. This time it was Mother Nature. In 1772, a hurricane devastated Saint Croix, prompting Hamilton to write a letter.

> Where now, oh! vile worm, is all thy boasted fortitude and resolution? What is become of thine arrogance and self sufficiency? Why dost thou tremble and stand aghast? How humble, how helpless, how contemptible you now appear. And for why? The jarring of elements—the discord of clouds? Oh! impotent presumptuous fool! how durst thou offend that Omnipotence, whose nod alone were sufficient to quell the destruction that hovers over thee, or crush thee into atoms? See

Omnipotence, whose nod alone were sufficient to quell the destruction that hovers over thee, or crush thee into atoms? See thy wretched helpless state, and learn to know thyself. Learn to know thy best support. Despise thyself, and adore thy God.

The excerpt highlights Hamilton's flare for the dramatic. When the letter was published, Hamilton became a minor local celebrity. The story goes that as a direct result of his creative writing, some businessmen took up a collection to send the young bard to New York where he could go to college. It *was* a good story, and it became the inspiration for Miranda: "I was like, This is an album—no, this is a show. . . . It was the fact that Hamilton wrote his way off the island where he grew up. That's the hip-hop narrative."

But that story might not be completely true. New research has shown that it was probably Hamilton's cousin, Ann Mitchell, who gave him the funds to go to New York. And it helps explain why, on the night before his famous duel with Aaron Burr, he wrote in a letter to his wife, "Mrs. Mitchell is the person in the world to whom as a friend I am under the greatest Obligations."

III. Abolitionist or Slaveholder?

Alexander Hamilton is often called an abolitionist, someone

who aims to end slavery. In an 1841 biography on Hamilton, his son John Church Hamilton wrote that his father "never owned a slave." But in a 1910 biography, Hamilton's grandson Allan McLane Hamilton argues that no, that's just not true. And new research backs McLane Hamilton up.

Hamilton was part of an effort to start encouraging people to free their own enslaved people. He was an important member of the New York Manumission Society, founded in part to help protect freed Black people in New York from being kidnapped back into slavery.

WHAT'S THE (RIGHT) WORD?

Manumission vs. Abolition

The goal of *abolition* was to end the Atlantic slave trade by outlawing it. *Manumission* was about transition, focusing on a gradual end to slavery by encouraging slaveholders to voluntarily emancipate the enslaved, rather than forcing people to do so through laws. The most famous case of manumission was that of Virginia plantation owner Robert Carter III, who freed over 450 enslaved people, giving many of them parcels of land.

The society advocated for An Act of the Gradual

Abolition of Slavery, passed into law in New York in 1799. The Act declared that any child born to an enslaved mother after July 4, 1799, would be legally free, but not until the men were age twenty-eight, women age twenty-five. (Talk about gradual.) Many of the Manumission Society's members were slaveholders, including fellow politicians Aaron Burr and John Jay, who was governor of New York at the time. More of that Founder hypocrisy: They believed slavery was abhorrent, or at least that it should eventually be outlawed, but they continued to practice it for their own personal gain. And they were clearly not in a hurry to end the practice. Was Hamilton also a slaveholder?

Ron Chernow, whose best-selling biography *Alexander Hamilton* is the basis for Miranda's Broadway show, concedes it's possible that Hamilton did enslave several people as an adult. But Chernow writes mostly on how Hamilton fought slavery, the good deeds of the Manumission Society, and how it was in Nevis and Saint Croix that Hamilton learned to hate slavery.

> The memories of his West Indian childhood left Hamilton with a settled antipathy [a strong dislike] to slavery. During the war, Hamilton had supported John Lauren's futile effort to

emancipate southern slaves who fought for independence. He had expressed an unwavering belief in the genetic equality of blacks and whites—unlike Jefferson, for instance, who regarded blacks as innately inferior—that was enlightened for his day. And he knew this from his personal boyhood experience.

Slavery was particularly brutal on the islands. Nevis and Saint Croix were paradoxes of spectacular beauty and extreme cruelty. In 1765, twenty-two thousand of the twenty-four thousand residents on Saint Croix were enslaved people. They had been kidnapped and shipped there to work in labor camps on sugar plantations and in the homes of the white minority. Even though the family didn't have much money, the Hamiltons did enslave more than a few boys as household laborers, so Hamilton was personally exposed to slavery as a child.

Maybe Hamilton saw slavery as an evil because of his childhood, as Chernow and other biographers have claimed. But Jessie Serfilippi, a historical interpreter for the Schuyler Mansion in Albany, New York, doesn't agree. "I've looked into this as much as I could and there are no historical documents that suggest this," Serfilippi said in an interview with True History.

In fact, during the time Hamilton worked as a clerk at

the import/export firm Beekman and Cruger on Saint Croix, Serfilippi says the company was involved in at least one sale of hundreds of enslaved people per year. As a clerk, Hamilton would have worked on those transactions.

Serfilippi, who has done extensive research on Hamilton, says biographers tend to embrace the story of Hamilton as an abolitionist. Because he had a different childhood than his Revolutionary peers, biographers fall back on this theory that he was turned off to slavery on Saint Croix to help support the abolitionist narrative.

COOL CAREER

Historical Interpreter

Jessie Serfilippi is a *historical interpreter* for the Schuyler Mansion. What's that? Here's her answer: "A historical interpreter gives tours of a historic site and performs related research. The term *interpreter* acknowledges that when we give tours, we offer an interpretation of primary sources. A good interpreter isn't an all-knowing being but rather your starting point to learn more." It's a great job for someone who loves history, public speaking, writing, and research.

After two years of research into Hamilton's relationship to slavery, Serfilippi published a paper in 2020 called "'As Odious and Immoral a Thing': Alexander Hamilton's Hidden History as an Enslaver." She argues that Hamilton was not only a slaveholder as an adult but that he was hired to help buy enslaved people for others and consulted people on issues of slavery as a lawyer, making money through the institution. She says slavery was an essential part of his professional and personal identity.

Serfilippi says it's more likely that Hamilton's exposure to slavery as a child had a different effect on him than the one that biographers promote.

"If he was like most other white men in his time period, then he would have internalized that slaveholding was the road to success. For a lot of white people, and specifically white men because they were often the ones who held more power and could make more decisions, enslaving someone was a status symbol, as much as it was about having someone to work for you. It showed that you were successful and that you were part of the upper-class elite society."

HISTORY RECAP

Hamilton's career straddled multiple fields, and he racked

up lots of accomplishments in his short life. He only lived into his forties. He was a military commander in the Revolutionary War, a lawyer, a banker, and an aide to George Washington. He was Washington's first Treasury secretary and had a vital role in shaping the government, especially the economic policies of the country. Along with John Jay and James Madison, Hamilton wrote the **Federalist Papers**, eighty-five essays supporting the ratification of the Constitution. It was kind of like collaborating on a school project but doing most of the work yourself: Hamilton wrote fifty-one of them.

IV. On the Case

Serfilippi's research gets even more interesting when Hamilton marries into the wealthy Schuyler family in New York. Slavery was common throughout the state when Hamilton lived there. For example, in 1790, ten years after he married Elizabeth Schuyler, there were twenty-one thousand enslaved people recorded in New York.

Serfilippi spent time combing through Hamilton's cashbooks to look for evidence. Think of a cashbook like an online banking account: It shows earnings, purchases, bills paid, and who has received payment for services. While they might sound boring, cashbooks can actually tell us a quite interesting story.

In Hamilton's cashbooks, the laborers always receive "wages." These are people who did lawn work or were hired to be coachmen, for instance. But there is no record for wages paid to household help for cooking and cleaning—except for a woman who did the laundry. And people of the Hamiltons' stature would definitely have had people in the house doing this work.

It was common to call enslaved people "servants" in New York. The only cashbook entry in which Hamilton lists the "servants" receiving money is as a "donation." This is where Serfilippi did some real detective work.

She noticed that the donation to servants was made around the time of Easter and Pentecost. And she knew that it was also around the time of a Dutch holiday called Pinkster, celebrated in New York by people of African descent. Serfilippi found the date for Easter the year of the entry and then figured out when Pinkster would have been. And voilà! It all made sense that Hamilton had given gifts of small amounts of money to the people he enslaved to celebrate the holiday.

WHAT'S THAT WORD?

Pinkster was a celebration by people of African descent that began on Pentecost, seven weeks after Easter. Originally derived from Dutch celebrations, it became a time for both free and enslaved people to gather together and visit with family and friends. Pinkster revolved around African traditions, and it was a way for enslaved people to assert agency (to act independently and have freedom of choice) to celebrate the holiday following their own traditions. Pinkster is almost entirely unique to New York and especially the Hudson River Valley region.

There are other examples in the cashbooks of transactions involving enslaved persons. In 1796, Hamilton purchased a woman and child and paid his father-in-law for "2 Negro servants purchased by him for me." In 1798, Hamilton recorded receiving one hundred dollars (equivalent to almost $3,000 today) for "the return" of this child (someone under the age of twelve). Serfilippi says that means he sent the child out to another slaveholder and collected the money for the work the child did. He could not have done that if the child was not enslaved. "It happened often that enslavers collected money that the enslaved made, but knowing in this case it's a mother and child purchased together, and the child was sent away for a time from his mother, is really heartbreaking, to say the least."

In a summary of Hamilton's estate after he was killed by Aaron Burr, the summation of his property includes an entry for servants valued at hundreds of dollars. If they had not been enslaved, the servants wouldn't have been counted as property. Serfilippi considers that another important piece of evidence.

Serfilippi says one of the reasons the cashbooks became so important to her research is that she started to realize there were letters missing from the Hamilton archives that would have shed light on his relationship to slavery.

V. The Eyes of History

Although the Founders were definitely concerned with their own legacies, Serfilippi says in this case, it was likely Alexander's wife, Elizabeth, and son John Church Hamilton—not Alexander himself—who dumped the letters, in the years after he died, to protect his name: "The world has completely shifted around them, and they recognize that this legacy of enslaving people is not good for Hamilton. So it's written out of the narrative, and I think that's why these letters, that would have been very useful, are missing."

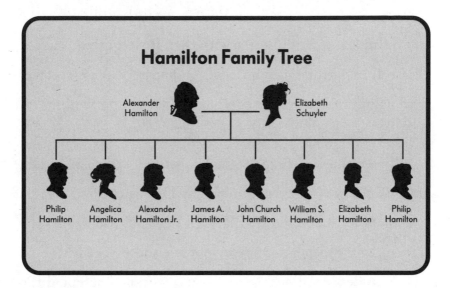

Hamilton Family Tree

Alexander Hamilton — Elizabeth Schuyler

Philip Hamilton · Angelica Hamilton · Alexander Hamilton Jr. · James A. Hamilton · John Church Hamilton · William S. Hamilton · Elizabeth Hamilton · Philip Hamilton

Why look at what's missing from the record? Why look back at all, at a life written about many times, and dredge up evidence that paints Hamilton in a negative light, less than a decade after a Broadway show gave him celebrity status? Serfilippi says if we don't present history accurately, we are "doomed to repeat it, even if not the same exact way, [in] similar ways."

The most important issue for her was acknowledging the people who Hamilton enslaved and placing them in his story, where they belong. Without them, Serfilippi says, the story is incomplete. "If we portray [Hamilton] as he truly was, we don't contribute to the mythology surrounding him and slavery. And we can say, he did extraordinary things. . . . I don't think anyone will argue with that. But we can talk about those things while acknowledging that he was an enslaver and acknowledging the people he enslaved and working to learn as much about them as we can."

Lin-Manuel Miranda faced some criticism when *Hamilton* was released as a movie by Disney in 2020. While the show features a mostly Black and Latino cast playing the roles of white men and women, it barely addresses the issue of the Founders' relationship to slavery. Miranda accepted the criticism and said it was valid.

"Hamilton—although he voiced anti-slavery beliefs— remained complicit in the system." And Miranda said, "Other than calling out Jefferson on his hypocrisy with regards to slavery in Act 2, [Hamilton] doesn't really say much else over the course of Act 2. And I think that's actually pretty honest. . . . He didn't really do much about it after that. None of them did. None of them did enough."

Miranda is right: None of the Founders did enough about

slavery.

Up next: an American who spent his adult life in the abolitionist movement.

LET'S TALK ABOUT IT

* Serfilippi's discoveries about Hamilton are recent. Do you think it's important for historians to continue to study historical figures even after there have been so many books and papers written about them? Why or why not?

* Why do you think Lin-Manuel Miranda cast mostly people of color to play white historical figures in his musical *Hamilton*?

CHAPTER 5
"WHAT TO THE SLAVE IS THE FOURTH OF JULY?": FREDERICK DOUGLASS

You might be wondering why Frederick Douglass—an American abolitionist born into slavery in 1818—is included in a book about the men and women from an earlier era. The reason? His story and his words provide a source of reflection on the men of the Revolutionary era. And some of his words still resonate today. Douglass also gives us a framework to ask an important question: Will the United States ever be able to fully live up to those ideals in the Declaration of Independence?

Like Alexander Hamilton, Douglass was a young man when he became known as a brilliant orator. Having learned to read and write as a child, he had the skills to tell his harrowing story, which was uncommon for a person who had spent his youth enslaved.

In the second of three autobiographies, Frederick Douglass recalls when he started to think about the conditions of his life as a child. He had been separated from his mother so early that he had little memory of seeing her. He knew his father was a white man, rumored to be the cruel master of the plantation where the enslaved Douglass worked and lived with his grandmother. And as a young boy, he wondered why this was his life.

> *Why am I a slave? Why are some people slaves, and other masters? Was there ever a time when this was not so?* . . . Once, however, engaged in the inquiry, I was not very long in finding out the true solution of the matter. It was not *color*, but *crime*, not *God*, but *man*, that afforded the true explanation of the existence of slavery; nor was I long in finding out another important truth, viz: what man can make, man can unmake . . .

A CLOSER LOOK

When researching men like Jefferson who fathered children with the women they enslaved, the question comes up often: How did they treat those children? The answer varies from slaveholder to slaveholder, but

Frederick Douglass explains why so many of them were cruel to their children.

Men do not love those who remind them of their sins—unless they have a mind to repent [express regret]—and the mulatto [mixed-race] child's face is a standing accusation against him who is master and father to the child. What is still worse, perhaps, such a child is a constant offense to the wife. She hates its very presence.

Douglass did not wait for man to unmake the existence of slavery. In 1838, when he was about twenty years old and living as an enslaved man in Baltimore, he met a free Black woman named Anna Murray. Frederick fell in love with Anna, who encouraged him to seek his own freedom, and she helped him get to New York, which had outlawed slavery in 1827.

Disguised as a sailor, he took a train, then a steamboat and another train, arriving in New York about twenty-four hours later. New York City isn't that far from Baltimore, but it might as well have been another planet for Douglass, who later reflected on his first day as a free man.

A new world had opened upon me. If life is more than breath, and the "quick round of blood," I lived more in one day than in a year of my slave life. It was a time of joyous excitement which words can but tamely describe.

NAME CHANGE

Frederick Douglass was born Frederick Augustus Washington Bailey. When he escaped slavery, he changed his name to Frederick Douglass, after a character in a Walter Scott poem. (He added an extra s.) He did it to avoid recapture but also to give himself a fresh start—a new identity. And maybe, just maybe, he wanted to ditch the name *Washington*.

Douglass was born in 1818, about fourteen years after Hamilton died and forty-two years after the signing of the Declaration of Independence. Douglass did not know the actual day of his birthday but later adopted February 14 as the day.

Can you imagine not knowing when you were born? He writes in his first autobiography, *Narrative of the Life of Frederick Douglass*, that white children always knew their ages, but he did not.

> By far the larger part of the slaves know as little of their ages as horses know of theirs, and it is the wish of most masters within my knowledge to keep their slaves thus ignorant. I do not remember to have ever met a slave who could tell of his birthday.

Douglass could have been born a free man if Jefferson's antislavery diatribe against the king or other antislavery language had been included in the Declaration and the new nation had acted to abolish slavery, even gradually. But he was born enslaved, in what is now Cordova, Maryland, during the Monroe administration.

HISTORY RECAP

James Monroe, the fifth president of the United States, was the last of the Founders to be president. He was also a slaveholder, yet another labor camp owner from Virginia. Like most of his peers, he claimed to believe that slavery was wrong but continued the practice even as the tides were turning in the northern states, where laws were passed to abolish it.

Douglass had the experience of growing up enslaved in the horrendous environment of labor camps as well as the relatively better environs of a city. And he lived most of his adult life as a free man. Those vastly different experiences enabled him to tell a powerful and moving story rarely heard from a formerly enslaved person.

In 1841, Douglass and Anna, now his wife, were living in New Bedford, Massachusetts, when he took a ferry to the island of Nantucket to hear the well-known abolitionist William Lloyd Garrison speak. After Garrison's remarks, a friend from New Bedford asked Douglass to tell his personal story.

Just twenty-three years old, Douglass was nervous. It was the first time he had spoken to a white audience. But he blew everyone away with his impromptu and impassioned words. As one person present said, "Flinty [hard and unyielding] hearts were pierced, and cold ones melted by his eloquence."

In addition to an incredible story, Douglass had natural star power. "Douglass embodied the reality, confounding [confusing in a surprising way] to racists, that a black man could be charismatic, imposing, educated, and a voice for absolute emancipation," Adam Gopnik writes in the *New Yorker* magazine.

Garrison realized he had found the man he'd been looking for—someone to put a face and voice to the abolition movement. The two formed a partnership that would greatly further the abolitionist cause over the next dozen years and redefine the mission of Douglass's life.

II. Not My Holiday

Fast-forward to the summer of 1852. It's seventy-six years after the signing of the Declaration of Independence and nine years until the Civil War breaks out. Frederick Douglass is now a famous journalist, author, and speaker. He stands before an audience in Rochester, New York, to give one of the most impassioned speeches on the subject of slavery ever recorded. It has become known as his "What to the Slave Is the Fourth of July?" speech.

Douglass starts his address with words of respect for the "fathers of this republic," who he says were brave men. "It does not often happen to a nation to raise, at one time, such a number of truly great men." And maybe with these first sentences, Douglass's audience is lulled into thinking this will be a speech celebrating this remarkable day in US history. He has chosen the word "great" to describe the Founders.

In Douglass's estimation, the Founders deserve neither straightforward praise nor full condemnation. "The point from which I am compelled to view them is not, certainly, the most favorable; and yet I cannot contemplate their great deeds with less than admiration." At once, this is both the voice of a man who has been shunned by the Founders'

THE FOUNDERS

George Washington

Thomas Jefferson

Benjamin Franklin

Alexander Hamilton

James Madison

John Jay

John Adams

These seven men are generally considered the Founders.

PORTRAITS OF PRESIDENTS (1–18)

1. George Washington

2. John Adams

3. Thomas Jefferson

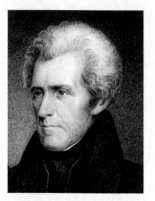

7. Andrew Jackson

8. Martin Van Buren

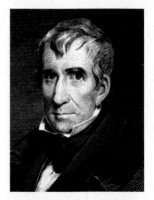

9. William Henry Harrison

13. Millard Fillmore

14. Franklin Pierce

15. James Buchanan

Names in red indicate presidents who enslaved people.

4. James Madison

5. James Monroe

6. John Quincy Adams

10. John Tyler

11. James K. Polk

12. Zachary Taylor

16. Abraham Lincoln

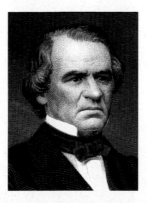

17. Andrew Johnson

18. Ulysses S. Grant

THE CONSTITUTION OF THE UNITED STATES

DRAFTING OF THE DECLARATION OF INDEPENDENCE

Engraving of Benjamin Franklin, Thomas Jefferson, and John Adams drafting the Declaration of Independence.

Engraving from 1823

MONTICELLO, VIRGINIA, HOME OF THOMAS JEFFERSON

From *A Popular History of the United States*
by W. C. Bryant and S. H. Gay, 1880

DUEL BETWEEN AARON BURR AND ALEXANDER HAMILTON

The Burr-Hamilton duel was fought at Weehawken, New Jersey, between
Vice President Aaron Burr and Alexander Hamilton on July 11, 1804.

A PORTRAIT OF
FREDERICK DOUGLASS

Vintage portrait of Frederick Douglass (1818–1895), an American
social reformer, abolitionist, orator, writer, and statesman. After
escaping from slavery in Maryland in 1838, he became a national
leader of the abolitionist movement in Massachusetts and New York.

actions, because of the color of his skin, and the voice of the journalist, who can see their work with some objectivity.

But Douglass recognizes throughout the remainder of the speech that the Founders' accomplishments had nothing to do with his life, as a Black man.

Douglass asks the audience why he has been invited to speak at an event commemorating the signing of the Declaration of Independence. After all, in 1852, millions of Black Americans were still enslaved in the South. Most Black Americans were not able to enjoy life, liberty, and the pursuit of happiness.

"What have I, or those I represent, to do with your national independence?" He does not hold back.

> The rich inheritance of justice, liberty, prosperity and independence, bequeathed [given] by your fathers, is shared by you, not by me. The sunlight that brought light and healing to you, has brought stripes [imprisonment] and death to me. This Fourth July is yours, not mine. You may rejoice, I must mourn. To drag a man in fetters [chains] into the grand illuminated temple of liberty, and call upon him to join you in joyous anthems, were inhuman mockery and sacrilegious irony. Do you mean, citizens, to mock me, by asking me to speak to-day?

Douglass is asking his audience: Did they invite him there to make fun of him? He sees great irony in the fact that they have asked him to come to speak about the country's liberation from Great Britain when so many Black people are still enslaved in the country. He is telling them that they, as white Americans, have reason to celebrate that day; he does not.

It is worth the time to read this speech in its entirety, as Douglass blasts the hypocrisy of the Declaration of Independence and the nation that so proudly embraces it. He states bluntly that he is not going to argue the case against slavery, as that would be ridiculous. The truth is already known to all.

"There is not a man beneath the canopy of heaven that does not know that slavery is wrong for him." And he says it is well past time to do something about it.

> The feeling of the nation must be quickened; the conscience of the nation must be roused; the propriety of the nation must be startled; the hypocrisy of the nation must be exposed; and its crimes against God and man must be proclaimed and denounced.

It is impossible to understand fully what Douglass must have felt in that moment, still waiting for the country to abolish slavery nationwide; still unable to convince the South to wake up; still fighting for the freedom of Black men, women, and children enslaved by whites who would beat them, hunt them down with dogs, and sell them on the auction block. The president of the United States at the time, northerner Millard Fillmore, had signed the Fugitive Slave Act into law and did not act to amend it to protect free people from being kidnapped and sold into slavery in the South.

HISTORY RECAP

The **Fugitive Slave Act** of 1850 required that enslaved people who had escaped must be returned to their owners, even if they were caught in states where slavery was outlawed. And it required that people in freed states cooperate. Abolitionists called it the "Bloodhound Bill" after the dogs that were used to track runaways. The act also made the federal government responsible for finding and returning enslaved persons and putting them on trial.

How then, argues Douglass, is the Fourth of July a holiday for Black people?

What, to the American slave, is your 4th of July? I answer; a day that reveals to him, more than all other days in the year, the gross injustice and cruelty to which he is the constant victim. To him, your celebration is a sham; your boasted liberty, an unholy license; your national greatness, swelling vanity; your sounds of rejoicing are empty and heartless; your denunciation of tyrants, brass fronted impudence; your shouts of liberty and equality, hollow mockery; your prayers and hymns, your sermons and thanksgivings, with all your religious parade and solemnity, are, to Him, mere bombast, fraud, deception, impiety, and hypocrisy—a thin veil to cover up crimes which would disgrace a nation of savages. There is not a nation on the earth guilty of practices more shocking and bloody than are the people of the United States, at this very hour.

There is a lot to unpack here. Douglass is saying that to enslaved people, July 4 is not a day of celebration. Rather, it is a reminder of how terribly they have been treated by the United States. It is a sad day. He says when the United States claims to be morally superior to other countries, when Americans brag that their country is rooted in freedom for all men, enslaved Americans know that those claims are lies. And he says the United States, on that day, in that year, is guilty of more violent and cruel behavior than any other country in the world.

Douglass spoke truth to power in a way that few people had ever spoken about the country and its white supremacy and hypocrisies. And his words resonate today with those who have been oppressed, incarcerated, or killed in this country because of their race, their gender or sexual orientation, religion, immigration status, or their poverty.

And yet, will it shock you to learn that toward the end of the speech, Douglass defends this same nation? Coming full circle to his opening, with admiration for the Founders' accomplishments, he says he does "not despair of this country."

In the twenty-first century, when police brutality against Black people sparked a wave of Black Lives Matter protests, and so much of the legacy of slavery and racial division in this country is still on glaring display, it is startling to read that Frederick Douglass had hope for the country a full 150 years earlier, in the era of slavery. But he believed that "the doom of slavery" was certain. Even he, a formerly enslaved man, drew hope from the Declaration of Independence and "the great principles it contains."

Douglass founded an antislavery newspaper called *The North Star*, which he published from 1847 to 1860. And from 1861 till 1865, he was a consultant to President Lincoln during the Civil War. He lived to see slavery abolished, and throughout Reconstruction, he fought for the civil rights of freed people, and he supported the women's rights movement until the end of his life.

The breadth of his accomplishments is incredible for any man. But it is astonishing for a man who was born enslaved, for a boy who didn't even know the date of his birth, to come so far in one lifetime. Frederick Douglass had an extraordinary impact on the United States and the fights for racial equality and women's equality. And he gave Black Americans, and all Americans hoping to see slavery end, a sense of optimism that the United States could and would live up to its promise.

HISTORY RECAP

The **Reconstruction era** was the period from 1865 to 1877 that refers to the rebuilding of the country after the Civil War. In those years the United States wrestled with issues of reintegrating the Southern states into the Union and the legal status of Black Americans. It was during this time that the Thirteenth, **Fourteenth**, and Fifteenth Amendments were added to the Constitution, giving Black Americans more rights under the law. (See Chapter 7 for more on the Constitution.)

To see James Earl Jones, the actor who voices Darth Vader in *Star Wars*, read the "What to the Slave Is the Fourth of July?" speech in its entirety, go to the Further Readings section for a link to the video.

* Do you think the United States can live up to the ideals laid out in the Declaration of Independence, that all men (all people) are created equal?

* Why do you think Native Americans often criticize Columbus Day and Thanksgiving as holidays they do not wish to celebrate?

CHAPTER 6
FLAWED HERO:
GEORGE WASHINGTON

Murals of George Washington cover 1,600 square feet of walls in the hallways of George Washington High School in San Francisco. In thirteen different scenes, the painter sometimes shows Washington in a critical light. There are two paintings that are particularly controversial. In one, Washington is standing with some of the Founders on a platform, pointing westward. A dead Native American lies on the ground, facedown; soldiers with rifles walk over him. In another, Washington is standing to the side listening to a white overseer who is pointing toward enslaved Black men, who are shucking corn and bagging cotton.

The murals were commissioned in 1935 as part of President Franklin Delano Roosevelt's Federal Art Project for public buildings. They were created by a Russian émigré artist named Victor Arnautoff, a protégé of the famous Mexican painter Diego Rivera. (Rivera was married to artist Frida Kahlo.) Arnautoff's murals—and the racism they highlight—have been the source of a decades-long debate that erupted in and out of the school community in 2019.

HISTORY RECAP

FDR's **Federal Art Project** was a New Deal program to fund the work of visual artists in the United States. It was created to employ artists and artisans after the Great Depression to create murals, sculpture, paintings, posters, photography, and more. The **New Deal** was a series of public works projects and financial reforms to prevent another depression. It was enacted by FDR from 1933–1939 to restart the US economy and get Americans back to work.

Some of the students and parents at George Washington High School wanted the murals to be painted over because the kids didn't want to see the images every day. They said the paintings reinforced stereotypes. One student talked about being tired of hearing, "I'll meet you at the dead Indian."

Art historians and others in the community argued that the murals are important pieces of art that should be preserved, as they are a part of US history. In the end, the school board voted to cover the paintings with panels but leave them on the walls, which didn't really make anybody happy.

One art historian who took an interest in the debate said that he understood why students of color would be upset by the images. But he pointed out that it is a missed educational opportunity. There are no plaques and no school orientation explaining the paintings, which can be seen as a critique of both white America's western expansion and of Washington himself.

The twenty-first-century question of how to treat the revered men central to the founding of the country is one that splits the country—sometimes along racial lines, sometimes generationally, and often along political lines. (Remember the Robert E. Lee statue from Chapter 2?) And George Washington's name is frequently brought up as a sort of dividing line in itself.

The story of George Washington High School is interesting because the art in question looks at Washington critically; it does not whitewash his story. And some say removing the art would do just that.

WHAT DOES *THAT* MEAN?

To **whitewash** something is to deliberately conceal or cover up a fault or something dishonest, immoral, or even illegal. In the case of history, it usually means to conceal history that is ugly or hard—and often the word is literal. Whitewashing can mean that an event in history is told from a white perspective, concealing the parts of the story that reflect negatively on white people and ignoring the oppression experienced by minorities.

Sometimes the question is less about whether such monuments and artwork should be removed in total and more about whether they should be removed from a particular place.

Some argue, though, that art should make people feel uncomfortable. But others at the high school say that as they go to class, children of color should not have to look at reminders of a history based on slavery and genocide, making them uncomfortable every day.

Here's a look at some of the history in those paintings.

II. Devourer of Villages

The accounts of Washington's victories on the battlefield are well documented in textbooks. (He actually racked up more losses than wins.) And his battles against Indigenous people, once regarded as victories, look very different in a contemporary light.

In 1753 Seneca leader Tanacharison nicknamed Washington "Conotocarius," which means "devourer of villages" or "town taker." The name had been given to Washington's great-grandfather in the seventeenth century, and when Tanacharison met George, he revived it. It was premature, but Washington would live up to the title.

When Washington was first cutting his military teeth on the French and Indian War, he actually grew to appreciate Indigenous peoples' military skills. Later, as a general during the Revolutionary War, he even adopted some of the war tactics he had previously observed.

HISTORY REWRITE

Forget the Wooden-Teeth Story

School children are often taught the myth that George Washington had wooden dentures, part of the lore that surrounds the first president. He did have really bad teeth, and by the time he was sixty, only one of the teeth in his mouth was his. Washington was a vain man—so it's not surprising that he would spend money on dentures.

Washington biographer Alexis Coe writes in *You Never Forget Your First*, "At best, we can say that Washington had a poacher's smile." What she means is that his dentist sometimes took chunks of animal ivory to carve teeth for him.

But some of Washington's dentures have an even more sinister root. He often used human teeth to replace his, taking the teeth of people he enslaved. He would pay for them but only about a third of the value of teeth on the open market. It's no surprise that children are taught about the wooden teeth instead.

Washington had a complicated relationship with Indigenous people. At times, they fought beside him. Sometimes he sought their lands for his own personal gain. In other situations, Native Americans were his enemy, and he preached genocide: "The immediate objects are the total destruction and devastation of their settlements and the capture of as many prisoners of every age and sex as possible," he wrote in a letter to Major General John Sullivan in 1779.

That command for "total destruction" led to the Clinton-Sullivan Campaign during the Revolutionary War. On Washington's orders, Patriots burned more than forty villages and destroyed 160,000 bushels of corn crops. The bushels belonged to the tribes of the Iroquois Nation (Haudenosaunee) who had sided with the Loyalists, mostly in the Finger Lakes region of what is now upstate New York and Pennsylvania.

Washington instructed Major General Sullivan not to accept offers of peace from the Iroquois "before the total ruin of their settlements is effected . . ."

Approximately five thousand Native Americans escaped north to Canada to seek protection from the British, and others went to what is now Oklahoma and Wisconsin. The number of Indigenous people killed during this campaign is unknown. But the death toll from starvation and exposure to harsh winter weather was greater than losses in battle. And the campaign destroyed the Haudenosaunee's infrastructure.

The campaign was intended to put an end to Loyalist attacks on frontier settlements, like the Cherry Valley

Massacre in 1778, when thirty settlers were killed at the hands of Loyalist and Indigenous troops. Indigenous peoples' attacks on American settlers started again a year later and lasted through 1781. But the Clinton-Sullivan Campaign did significant permanent damage to the Haudenosaunee.

The campaign was a win for the colonies in another respect. In an exclusive interview with True History, Professor Jeffrey Ostler says, "Part of it is a war to undermine British positions and to undermine the Haudenosaunee support of the British. But it's also a war to get Haudenosaunee land, and there's no question of that. That really demonstrates that one of the animating forces behind independence is to get native lands."

Washington didn't think Native American life was compatible with colonial life. As president, Washington believed that Indigenous people could either assimilate (become part of settler colonial culture) or face extinction. He was not alone in that idea. Many of his peers agreed. But even if Indigenous people wanted to become part of the new country and live side by side with the colonists, the settlers made assimilation virtually impossible in most cases.

Ostler says, "I don't think that white Americans of this

time period could envision the possibility of living alongside Native Americans permanently if what that meant was Native Americans [living] on their own lands and having some degree of political autonomy [to be self-governed]. They could imagine incorporating Indigenous people into the dominant society as individuals, not as Indigenous people."

White settler colonialists considered themselves civilized and often considered Indigenous people to be "savages," the way Jefferson described them. They could not fathom the possibility of living near Indigenous people, and they did not want them in their midst. Someone had to go, and in the eyes of the settler colonialists, it wasn't going to be them.

Fast forward to the twenty-first century, and now it's Washington who is forced to go. Remember that high school in San Francisco with the controversial murals? In 2021, the city's school board voted to change the names of forty-four schools, including George Washington High School and even a school named after Abraham Lincoln. Again, this was another highly controversial decision that made national headlines. The school board said it was changing the names of schools named for historical figures linked to enslavement, oppression of women, genocide, and others who diminished the "opportunities of those amongst us to the right to life, liberty, and the pursuit of happiness."

III. Setting a Presidential Precedent

George Washington is often credited with being the only Founder to free the people he enslaved, which he did in his will. (More on that later.) This is not entirely accurate. Some Founders, like Benjamin Franklin, freed their enslaved persons before they died, so there was no need to put them in their wills. (Franklin only enslaved two people.) And freeing people in his will does not absolve Washington for his enduring relationship to slavery. He had the power to do much more. Washington was the first, but twelve presidents of the United States enslaved people at some time in their lives or throughout their lives. See the photo insert for a full list of these presidents.

Washington inherited ten enslaved people at the age of eleven when his father died. As a young man and plantation owner who purchased many more Africans, Washington didn't seem to have any issues or doubts about slavery. His wife, Martha Dandridge Custis, brought even more enslaved people to Mount Vernon, their home. Later in life, he told people that he didn't want to be a slaveholder anymore. But the motivations may have been primarily economic, at least at first. By the 1770s, Washington found that the profits from his labor camp did not cover the costs of feeding and clothing the people enslaved to work the land.

WHERE'S THAT?

Mount Vernon is a National Historic Landmark on the banks of the Potomac River in Fairfax County, Virginia. The site is one of the most visited historic sites in the United States. Mount Vernon was not only George and Martha's home, but it was also a working labor camp. The main house was built by his father, but when Washington took over the residence, he expanded it to a twenty-one-room mansion. At the time he lived there, the property included eight thousand acres. Like Jefferson, Washington first planted tobacco and then switched to wheat crops. Corn, vegetables, and grasses were also grown there.

Washington claimed to be against the practice of selling enslaved persons. But according to author Coe, at least three times he sold people to the West Indies, where they would likely work in labor camps on sugar plantations. He was well aware that this would be an awful life change for them.

Washington did have personal reservations about slavery after the Revolutionary War. In a 1786 letter, he writes:

> I never mean (unless some particular circumstances should compel me to it) to possess another slave by purchase; it being among my first wishes to see some plan adopted, by the legislature by which slavery in this Country may be abolished by slow, sure, & imperceptable [sic] degrees.

Again, like so many of the other Founders, Washington publicly favors gradual emancipation but leaves it to future generations to figure out.

After the war, Washington did stop buying and selling enslaved people. But in 1782, when he had the chance to free them under a new manumission law, he didn't do it.

For someone who increasingly expressed an unease with slavery, Washington's actions as president defy logic. With the capital of the new country moved from New York City to Philadelphia in 1790, for his second term his role as a slaveholder presented a difficult problem. Pennsylvania law guaranteed enslaved people the right to seek their freedom if they stayed in that state for more than six months.

Margaret Kimberley writes in her book, *Prejudential: Black America and the Presidents*, "This could have put Washington in a bind, but he had a solution: He rotated his human property for six-month intervals between Pennsylvania and Virginia. He did this in flagrant violation of a 1788 amendment to this law, which prohibited such actions."

REMEMBER THEIR NAMES

Ona Judge was one of the enslaved people rotated in and out of Philadelphia by the Washingtons. While in Philadelphia, Judge successfully escaped by boarding a ship headed for Portsmouth, New Hampshire. The Washingtons tried multiple times to recapture her, but they were unsuccessful. Judge told her story to two New Hampshire newspapers at the end of her life, nearly fifty years after she escaped, long after George and Martha Washington were dead.

At the time of his death, Washington enslaved 317 people. In a will he drew up in 1799 at the end of his presidency, he provided for the emancipation of the 123 enslaved people he owned outright. But this didn't include the dower slaves his wife Martha had inherited from her first husband, Daniel Parke Custis. (Neither Martha nor George could legally free them.)

There was a major caveat: Washington's will stated that

the enslaved people wouldn't actually be freed until after his wife's death. Martha worried that made her a target for murder, so a year after her husband died at age sixty-seven, she freed them.

WHAT'S THAT WORD?

Dower comes from the word *widower*. Martha's first husband died, leaving her a widow and giving her lifetime use of one-third of the Custis enslaved population.

Freeing his enslaved persons but not hers created a tragic problem. The two groups of people who had lived together for decades—many were married and had children together—were now separated.

IV. The Hero

George Washington is the Founder young people know the most about—mostly the good. Ultimately, he rises above the less flattering history in many accounts to be an American hero: the gallant general seen crossing the Delaware, the revered father of the country, and the man who set the standard for its leadership. The height of the Washington

Monument in DC (555 feet and 5⅛ inches) is testament to his legacy. So are the countless streets, statues, schools, buildings, and people named for him.

WHAT'S IN A NAME?

Washington

Kimberley says 90 percent of the Washingtons in the United States are Black people. It's impossible to know how many of them are actually descended from Washington and how many picked the name themselves.

"Most of the ancestors of today's Washingtons probably chose the name as a way of identifying themselves with their country, a major irony in the face of what Black people have had to contend with throughout this country's history."

Historian Stephen Ambrose once wrote that Washington is responsible for the "We can do it" American spirit. He says he personified the word *great* "in his ability to persuade, in his sure grip on what the new nation needed (above all else, not a king), and in his optimism no matter how bad the American cause looked, he rose above all others."

His leadership as the country's first president should never be taken away from him. Nor should his heroics in battle and forty years of military service. But there is more to the story, and it's a complex one that requires more introspection or self-examination as a country.

Ostler says there's an American contingent that argues that when we talk about uglier historical truths, we undermine the United States as a people; that those conversations and revelations divide us and pit us against each other. But he disagrees: "The only way we're going to get to a point where we can have any really deeply meaningful democracy and national community, where all the members of the nation have really an equal role, a seat at the table, is to reckon with the fact that that's never happened before and to understand why . . . We still have systemic racism, and we need to understand why we still have it. Unless we really understand that, I don't think we're going to be able to get beyond where we are now."

In other words, before all the stakeholders in the country can share equally in US democracy—something that has yet to be achieved—we must first understand the history that explains why we haven't been able to achieve it.

Kimberley argues that if you're going to tell the true

story of Washington and the other Founders, you must also tell it from the perspective of Black Americans. "When you leave out the people who are descended from the enslaved, you leave out a huge part of the story. If you don't have that perspective, then you're telling lies. It's very simple. So if you write about Washington in Philadelphia, and you don't write about the fact that he rotated the people he owned, then you've told a lie. An omission [something left out] is still a lie. Omissions are no less acceptable than saying something which is factually untrue. So that is why it's important to have Black people especially telling the story of American history."

The country was not only founded by the men we call the Founders and other white settlers but by the millions of Black Americans who built the country brick by brick—while also contributing to the the country's cultural foundations—and by the Indigenous people who were in America for centuries before Europeans arrived. Without their perspectives, the story of America is incomplete and inaccurate.

LET'S TALK ABOUT IT

* In Chapter 2, Annette Gordon-Reed says that when it comes to taking down statues, she distinguishes between those who fought to secede from the country, like Confederate General Robert E. Lee, and those who sought to create a country, like George Washington, or later unite it, like Abraham Lincoln. What do you think should be done with statues and monuments to people like George Washington? Should they be left standing or removed? Does it make a difference where they are located?

* Do you think the name *George Washington* should be removed from schools and other public buildings?

CHAPTER 7
HARD HISTORY:
JAMES MADISON AND
THE CONSTITUTION

The first time Professor Hasan Kwame Jeffries visited Montpelier, the "haunting beauty" of James Madison's home in Virginia took his breath away. Jeffries says it was a beautiful but cold January day, right around Dr. Martin Luther King Jr.'s birthday.

On the approach to Madison's estate, Jeffries says you don't see anything until you cross railroad tracks, and then the former plantation—now a National Historic Landmark— unfolds before you. But it's not simply a gorgeous landscape.

"That's part of that haunting beauty because you're thinking, *this really is pretty*, but you know what happened there." Jeffries says you can't separate the beauty from the reality that it was a place where people were born in bondage and died in bondage. "And so it takes your breath away in a couple of different ways."

Professor Jeffries was given a tour of the estate. Inside the main house, he saw Madison's library—the centerpiece of the house and the room where Madison conceptualized the Bill of Rights. And then his guide took him to the basement, where he asked Jeffries to run his hands along a brick wall. At first, he didn't understand why.

"But then, I actually feel the impressions, these indentations in the face of the brick. And you kind of stop and look at it, it's kind of puzzling and it takes you a second to realize what they are. But then it becomes really apparent. These are actually fingerprints, handprints."

He says the bricks were made of clay and straw. (Picture when you're a kid in preschool, and you make a handprint in clay that hardens into a gift for your parents.)

"As they're making the brick, they're leaving their impressions. Totally accidental, it's just what they did. But when you realize that these are handprints, you're like, man, these were made by enslaved folk. You are literally touching slavery," Jefferies said in an exclusive interview with True History.

Jeffries noticed something unusual about the handprints: their small size. His guide explained that the bricks were made by enslaved children, ages six to eight. That was their job at Montpelier. Smaller children, as young as four, were responsible for picking up trash on the estate.

Jeffries, who is African American, immediately thought about his two young daughters. If they had been born at a different time, they might have been forced to make bricks instead of learning to read and write. He felt an instant connection to the people who had to toil so hard for one family's comfort.

"I was going through this range of emotion—sadness, shock, anger, surprise. And then it hits me that we just left the library where Madison spends several months. The only reason he was able to lock himself away is because he has everyone else doing all the work for him on this slave-labor camp."

Jeffries says he started thinking about what was created in that library. "The place where this foundational document comes into being. Foundational in that this is the Bill of

Rights, this is laying out our fundamental freedoms—everything that is supposed to be protected and sacred, that the government cannot take away is crafted in that library. And that library rests on a foundation of bricks made by the children that this guy enslaved. What do you do with that? You just sit with it for a while and you're like, man, this is American history."

It's that "hard history" that Jeffries talks about earlier in Chapter 2. He defines hard history as those aspects of America's past that typically involve people of color and other marginalized groups.

WHAT'S THAT WORD?

Marginalized refers to a group of people who are discriminated against and experience exclusion from the social, economic, and political seats of power. Marginalized people are often dismissed as less important.

"In this context, we're talking about race. Those aspects of our past, involving race, that make us uncomfortable about the present. James Madison had no problem enslaving children to make bricks for his comfort and convenience.

He's totally cool with that."

James Madison enslaved about one hundred people at Montpelier. He was also the Founder with the greatest impact on the crafting and ratifying of the US Constitution and the fourth president of the United States.

REMEMBER THEIR NAMES

Paul Jennings was one of the people Madison enslaved both at Montpelier and at the White House. He was born in 1799 to an enslaved woman who was the granddaughter of a Native American. His father was white. Jennings became Madison's manservant, enjoyed a relative amount of independence for an enslaved person, and learned to read and write.

Jennings wrote a memoir, *A Colored Man's Reminiscences of James Madison*, which is considered the first memoir about life at the White House. Though he writes very kindly about Madison and his wife, Dolley, Jennings had to negotiate and pay for his freedom. Years after James Madison died, Jennings had hoped Dolley would free him, but instead, she sold him for $200 to an insurance agent. The statesman Daniel Webster bought Jennings from the agent for $120 and allowed Jennings to pay off his freedom at $8 per month.

Dolley Madison lived in poverty in her later years. Jennings would occasionally visit her and give her small sums of his money.

II. The Founding Document

"We the People of the United States, in Order to form a more perfect Union," are some of the most recognizable words in the English language. Just about every American child learns the Preamble to the Constitution, and though most of us may not recall all fifty-two words of it, we remember this phrase.

The Preamble sets the stage for the Constitution and introduces the laws of the land. It tells us what the Founders intended this pivotal document to accomplish. And it declares that the provisions that follow are adopted by all citizens of the United States, "We the people." This is a Constitution meant for a unified nation rather than separate states.

But who wrote those lofty fifty-two words?

WORDS TO LIVE BY

The Preamble
"We the People of the United States, in Order to form a
more perfect Union, establish Justice, insure domestic

Tranquility, provide for the common defense, promote the general Welfare, and secure the Blessings of Liberty to ourselves and our Posterity, do ordain and establish this Constitution for the United States of America." Go to the photo insert to see the Constitution.

No . . . it wasn't Madison. Or Jefferson. Or Hamilton.

His name was Gouverneur Morris. Gouverneur was his first name—he was not a governor. Gouverneur Morris is considered a Founder. He signed the Articles of Confederation of 1778 when he was still in his twenties. He served as minister plenipotentiary to France from 1792 to 1794, and then represented New York in the US Senate from 1800 to 1803.

THE FORGOTTEN FOUNDER

Gouverneur Morris had a dramatic personal story punctuated by accidents and bad luck. When he was fourteen years old and already a student at King's College, now Columbia University, he accidentally knocked over a kettle of boiling water, scalding and scarring his right arm. He had to miss classes for a year.

When he was in his twenties, a carriage accident left Morris with a mangled ankle and broken bones. His regular doctor was out of town, and the doctors decided to cut off his leg below the knee. When his own doctor returned, he told him the amputation was unnecessary and the leg could have been saved.

The scarring and amputation may have something to do with why Morris never got much attention: He didn't fit the mold of the godlike Founder.

Morris died a pretty gruesome death. He suffered from a disease called gout, which caused him to have a urinary tract blockage. The pain must have been terrible, because he decided to clear the blockage himself. No, he was not a doctor. But he turned a piece of whalebone into a catheter. Instead, he inflicted more internal injuries on himself and died, at age sixty-four.

And he is credited with giving the Constitution not only its Preamble at the Constitutional Convention of 1787 but much of its finesse. He was a member of the Convention's five-man Committee of Style and Arrangement, but according to James Madison, it was Morris who stood out. "The finish given to the style and arrangement of the Constitution, fairly belongs to the pen of Mr. Morris," he wrote in a letter from 1831.

If Morris brought the style, James Madison was the man

behind the document that defines the United States. Madison is often called the "father of the Constitution" for his critical role in drafting it and generating support for it.

HISTORY RECAP

The **Constitution of the United States** is organized into three parts. Part one is the Preamble, part two is the Articles of the Constitution, and part three is the Amendments to the Constitution.

These are the seven articles:

Article I: The Legislative Branch—Creates a Congress to make laws; divides it into the Senate and House of Representatives; and lists its powers, including to check and balance the other two branches of government

Article II: The Executive Branch—Outlines the powers, roles, and terms of the president and vice president; provides for their removal through impeachment

Article III: The Judicial Branch—Establishes the US Supreme Court; authorizes Congress to establish federal courts

Article IV: The States—Outlines the relationship between the states and between the federal government and the states; outlines how new states can join the union

Article V: Amending the Constitution—Outlines the process for future generations to ratify (make official) amendments (changes) to the Constitution

Article VI: Supreme Law of the Land—Declares that the Constitution and the laws made from it are the highest laws of the land

Article VII: Ratification—Declares the Constitution official law once nine of thirteen states sign it

After the ratification of the Constitution, Madison became a well-respected leader in the House of Representatives and a close adviser to President Washington. In 1789, he took on the task of writing amendments to the Constitution. He was concerned with protecting individual rights against potential actions by the federal government and state legislatures. So he reviewed some two hundred proposals and various state constitutions and came up with nineteen constitutional amendments that he believed would make the states and the public happy. He campaigned hard among his political colleagues to get them ratified. In the end, President

Washington sent twelve of the amendments to the states—ten were approved by three-fourths of the states, enough votes to include them in the US Constitution. They would become known as the Bill of Rights.

But, of course, the protections enshrined in the Bill of Rights were not extended to all Americans. Professor Jeffries says the Bill of Rights really defined the country from the beginning, in more ways than you might think: "This is the starting point for us as a nation. This is the beginning. We often talk about slavery being America's original sin, but slavery is America's origin. . . . Our understanding of freedom is birthed in this moment. What Madison is able to enumerate [lay out, one by one] as these core freedoms for us as Americans, us today, is based on the freedom that he was denying to people he claimed ownership over. He understood the power of freedom of speech because he was denying it to the people he was claiming ownership over."

What exactly does Jeffries mean? He says to take the First Amendment, for example. Madison didn't allow enslaved people to speak freely or let them practice their own religion or petition government. Most enslaved people were denied any education, so they couldn't write their own newspapers.

HISTORY RECAP

The **Bill of Rights** is the first ten amendments to the Constitution, which guarantee Americans civil liberties, serve as the foundation for the rule of law in the United States, and guarantee the accused certain rights. Madison originally wrote nineteen amendments; ten were ratified in 1791. They are:

FIRST

- Freedom of speech
- Freedom of the press
- Freedom of religion
- Freedom of assembly
- Right to protest or petition the government

SECOND

- Right to bear arms

THIRD

- Protection against housing soldiers in civilian homes

FOURTH

- Protection against unreasonable search and seizure
- Protection against the issuing of warrants without probable cause

FIFTH

- Right to a fair trial
- Right that serious criminal charges must be started by a grand jury
- Protection against double jeopardy
- Protection against self-incrimination
- Protection against property seizure

SIXTH

- Right to a speedy and public trial
- Right to trial by an impartial jury
- Right to be informed of criminal charges
- Right to be confronted by witnesses
- Right to call witnesses

SEVENTH

- Right to trial by jury

EIGHTH

- Protection against excessive bail
- Protection against excessive fines
- Protection against cruel and unusual punishment

NINTH

- Rights granted in the Constitution shall not infringe on other rights

TENTH

- Powers not granted to the federal government in the Constitution belong to the states or the people

Even if they could, who would print them?

If this reminds you of Chapter 1 and the Declaration of Independence, it's because there are parallels. In both cases, highly intelligent men with big, brilliant ideas for a new nation—men who believed that, at its core, the United States should represent this grand idea of liberty—wrote enslaved people out of that liberty by not naming them. They allowed the institution of slavery to continue and flourish. The Constitution actually protected slaveholders (although this is a subject of debate among historians and constitutional law scholars) in these ways:

- The three-fifths compromise in Article I meant that three-fifths of "all other persons"—the enslaved population—would be added to a state's free population. This increased representation for Southern slave states in the House of Representatives, giving them more power and protecting slavery.

- The Constitution limited the ability of Congress to regulate the slave trade.

- It protected the "property" of Americans, which included human property.

- It allowed Congress to use militias to put down

insurrections, including slave rebellions.

- The Constitution forced states that had outlawed slavery to turn over enslaved people escaping from a slave state.

Neither the Declaration of Independence nor the Constitution protected the liberties of all people. But the Constitution would be amended again.

HISTORY RECAP

The Thirteenth and Fourteenth Amendments were ratified after the Civil War.

The **Thirteenth Amendment** abolished slavery. It states: "Neither slavery nor involuntary servitude, except as a punishment for crime whereof the party shall have been duly convicted, shall exist within the United States, or any place subject to their jurisdiction."

The **Fourteenth Amendment** protects all US citizens under the law. It states: "All persons born or naturalized in the United States, and subject to the jurisdiction thereof, are citizens of the United States and of the state wherein they reside. No state shall make or enforce any law which shall abridge the privileges or immunities of citizens of the United States; nor shall any state deprive any person of life, liberty, or property, without due process of law; nor deny to any person within its jurisdiction the equal protection of the laws."

The Founders themselves believed that the United States should adapt its laws to the time. This Jefferson quote is inscribed on the Jefferson Memorial in Washington, DC:

> I am not an advocate for frequent changes in laws and constitutions, but laws and institutions must go hand in hand with the progress of the human mind. As that becomes more developed, more enlightened, as new discoveries are made, new truths discovered and manners and opinions change, with the change of circumstances, institutions must advance also to keep pace with the times. We might as well require a man to wear still the coat which fitted him when a boy as civilized society to remain ever under the regimen of their barbarous ancestors.

Jefferson acknowledges here that in the future, Americans might see life in the eighteenth century as "barbarous," or brutal, cruel, uncivilized. While he does not think that laws should be changed frequently, he realizes that some of the laws that he and the other Founders have created will have to be altered eventually.

III. Origin and Legacy

Even though amendments abolishing slavery were added to the Constitution in the nineteenth century, Professor Jeffries says the brutal impact that the founding of the United States had on Black Americans didn't come to a screeching halt with their ratification. "This is our creation story. And then it doesn't end there. It then informs our form of government. How we understand, how we practice justice. This is who we are; it's our origin and it becomes who we are."

We still see the effects of those origins today in how justice is often carried out differently for Black Americans than whites, whether that's because of the prejudices of some police officers, prosecutors, and judges or because of laws that unfairly target people of color. For example, Black Americans have historically been punished much more severely for possession of marijuana, which is one of the reasons that so many states are changing their marijuana laws. This is just another example of systemic racism.

We can see the effects of that founding history when we talk about economic disparities between races and other opportunities for success that are often denied to Black Americans—and have been denied for generations. This is also systemic racism.

We see it in the way Black people have often been left out of the story of the country's founding because the history and legacy of slavery is painful, and it collides with the nostalgic stories of the nation's founding. But it's important to recognize the contributions of the enslaved people who literally built so much of the United States. It's important that their lives and humanity be acknowledged, as well as their struggles against brutal oppression and their accomplishments in spite of that oppression.

As Americans, we stand on the shoulders of people like Madison and Jefferson, Washington and Hamilton, and the other Founders.

"They laid the groundwork, they created an infrastructure for this nation, if you will. The Constitution and the Bill of Rights. We've been adding to it and defining it and redefining it, and building on what they left us. That's part of their legacy. So in that sense, I think we stand on their shoulders and aspire to reach higher," Jeffries says. "But it's not just the political giants on whose shoulders we stand. The foundation of this nation wasn't just laid by political thinkers, it was literally laid by enslaved folk, those little black boys and little black girls who Madison kept in bondage and had make bricks for him."

As Madison sat in his library and Jefferson sat in a room in Philadelphia, creating and writing these monumental documents, it was Black people held in bondage who did the physical labor to support them and build the physical foundations of the country.

There are many people who will say: Why must we talk about this? Yes, slavery was terrible—everyone knows that. But it's over now. Why do we have to reveal all of this negativity about the Founders?

"Because it's true. We're dealing with truth. It's as simple as that," Jeffries says. "If we don't understand how we got here, and acknowledge that we're still confronted with inequality, . . . then there's no way that you can address it effectively and efficiently."

He says we have to understand the structures and laws that have always been embedded in the country and that have created an unequal system for Black Americans from the start.

Some historians in this book have talked about how we don't want to repeat history, so we study and learn from it. Professor Jeffries has a somewhat different take.

"I very much think when we say 'repeating history' it gives us too much credit—until we stop doing the things at some point that created the inequality, and we haven't. And so this idea of learning about the past so that we can disrupt it, we can disrupt that continuum, we can stop doing the things that created inequality, that perpetuate inequality today, that's why we've got to understand what these guys were doing back then."

Jeffries says young people may not be making laws or deciding court cases yet, but someday they will be, and they will need to understand hard history. They—and you—need to know the truth in order to help make the country a more perfect union.

LET'S TALK ABOUT IT

* What kinds of amendments do you think might be added to the Constitution in the future?

* Can you think of actions by current or recent presidents, and Americans in general, that will someday be considered barbarous or unethical?

FURTHER READINGS

Chernow, Ron. *Alexander Hamilton*. New York: Penguin Books, 2005.

Coe, Alexis. *You Never Forget Your First: A Biography of George Washington*. New York: Penguin Books, 2021.

Dunbar, Erica Armstrong. *Never Caught: The Washingtons' Relentless Pursuit of the Runaway Slave, Ona Judge*. New York: Atria Books, 2017.

Ellis, Joseph J. *American Dialogue: The Founders and Us*. New York: Vintage Books, 2019.

Gordon-Reed, Annette. *The Hemingses of Monticello: An American Family*. New York: W. W. Norton & Company, Inc., 2008.

Kimberley, Margaret. *Prejudential: Black America and the Presidents*. Lebanon, NH: Steerforth Press, 2020.

Ostler, Jeffrey: *Surviving Genocide: Native Nations and the United States from the American Revolution to Bleeding Kansas*. New Haven: Yale University Press, 2019.

ONLINE READING

You can search for letters and other writings by the Founders here: https://founders.archives.gov/

Hemings, Madison, as told to S. F. Wetmore. *The Memoirs of Madison Hemings*. PBS, *Frontline: Jefferson's Blood*. Chronology. Aired May 2, 2000. https://www.pbs.org/wgbh/pages/frontline/shows/jefferson/cron/1873march.html.

Monticello website has a wealth of material on Thomas Jefferson and the people he enslaved. https://www.monticello.org/

Serfilippi, Jessie. *"As Odious and Immoral a Thing": Alexander Hamilton's Hidden History as an Enslaver*. Albany, NY: Schuyler Mansion State Historic Site, 2020. https://parks.ny.gov/documents/historic-sites/SchuylerMansionAlexanderHamiltonsHiddenHistoryasanEnslaver.pdf.

"The 1619 Project" published by the *New York Times Magazine* is full of excellent essays on the history and legacy of slavery. https://www.nytimes.com/interactive/2019/08/14/magazine/1619-america-slavery.html.

For related educational materials, visit "The 1619 Project Curriculum."
https://pulitzercenter.org/lesson-plan-grouping/1619-project-curriculum.

Washington's Mount Vernon website has lots of information about George
Washington, his family, and the people he enslaved.
https://www.mountvernon.org/

Zinn Education Project is primarily for teachers with tons of materials and
resources for teaching history from the people's perspective:
https://www.zinnedproject.org/

LISTENING AND VIEWING

Douglass, Frederick. "What to the Slave is the Fourth of July?" Read by James
Earl Jones. DemocracyNow.org. *The War and Peace Report*. YouTube video,
1.02. https://www.youtube.com/watch?v=O0baE_CtU08.

NPR's *Fresh Air* podcast offers an interview with *Hamilton* creator Lin-Manuel
Miranda. https://www.npr.org/2020/06/29/884691708/hamilton-creator-
lin-manuel-miranda.

NPR's *Hidden Brain: A Conversation About Life's Unseen Patterns* offers a podcast,
"The Founding Contradiction: Thomas Jefferson's Stance on Slavery."
https://www.npr.org/2020/06/29/884634146/the-founding-contradiction-
thomas-jeffersons-stance-on-slavery.

PBS's *Amanpour & Co.* offers a segment called "Annette Gordon-Reed on What
She Calls 'The American Dilemma.'" https://www.pbs.org/wnet/amanpour-
and-company/video/annette-gordon-reed-what-she-calls-american-
dilemma-d8dpro/.

TED: *Ideas Worth Spreading* offers a *TEDx Talk* by Hasan Kwame Jeffries, "Why
We Must Confront the Painful Parts of US History." https://www.ted.com/
talks/hasan_kwame_jeffries_why_we_must_confront_the_painful_parts_
of_us_history?language=en.